D1592680

THE OUTLOOK

FOR INTELLIGENCE

from

BOLLINGEN SERIES XLV

The Collected Works of Paul Valéry

Edited by Jackson Mathews

VOLUME 10

PAUL VALÉRY

THE OUTLOOK
FOR INTELLIGENCE

Translated by
Denise Folliot
and
Jackson Mathews

With a Preface by
François Valéry

BOLLINGEN SERIES XLV

PRINCETON UNIVERSITY PRESS

THIS BOOK WAS ORIGINALLY PUBLISHED IN 1962
AS PART I OF *HISTORY AND POLITICS*,
WHICH IS VOLUME TEN OF THE
COLLECTED WORKS OF PAUL VALÉRY
CONSTITUTING NUMBER XLV IN THE BOLLINGEN SERIES.
THIS SELECTION WAS FIRST PUBLISHED
BY HARPER & ROW, INC., IN 1963.

Library of Congress Cataloging-in-Publication Data
Valéry, Paul, 1871-1945.
The outlook for intelligence / Paul Valéry ; translated by
Denise Folliot and Jackson Mathews ; with a preface by François Valéry.
p. cm.—(Bollingen series ; 45)
(The collected works of Paul Valéry ; v. 10)
Originally published in 1962 by Bollingen Foundation
as pt. 1 of History and politics.
Bibliography: p. Includes index. ISBN 0-691-01881-2
1. Civilization. Modern—20th century. 2. Intellectual life.
I. Title. II. Series. III. Series: Valéry, Paul, 1871-1945.
Works. English. 1956 ; v. 10.
PQ2643.A26A23 vol. 10 [CB425]
848'.912091209 s—dc19 [909.82] 89-3802

Text designed by Andor Braun
Cover designed by Margaret Davis
Cover illustration: *Portrait of Valery*
by D'Espagnat, from the
Giraudon "Célébrités françaises" Collection,
reproduced with the permission of
Art Resource, New York.
Printed in the United States of America

CONTENTS

Preface

In HIS everyday life, Paul Valéry's appearance and habits were those of the average Frenchman. His respect for established social values allowed him to accept them with a deference surprising in a man with so strong a sense of his own worth— a man who was, for that matter, of excellent family, indeed of aristocratic origins on his mother's side. This patriotic Frenchman was born of an Italian mother and a Corsican father. Genoa, where one branch of his family had settled, was his favorite city; yet it was precisely from Genoa that, at the age of sixteen, he wrote to a friend: "You could never imagine how patriotic one feels the moment one is outside one's own country. I would never have believed I was so devoted to France." And he went on: "Nearly every day in the tram, I pass in front of an old house with a sign on the wall (I can see you beginning to smile): *Medical Dispensary for French Army Hospitals*. . . . You will see at once that these six common-place terms hold a world of memories, a vision of conquest and fame. . . ."

That schoolboy exulting in the memory of Napoleon never quite died in Valéry. "Patriot" is not strong enough— he was a chauvinist. At the sound of a military band passing in the street, he would fall into step. An individualist, he com-plained like all boys at having to do his military service (he was called up at the early age of eighteen); but he found a certain exhilaration in the disciplined life and even in the morning drill. Paul Valéry was unquestionably of a Catholic turn of mind, which he owed to his upbringing; but as a Catholic he was more than agnostic, he was a disbeliever.

One day he said to a Protestant friend of his, to tease him: "You Protestants are a lot of . . ." (here he used an unprintable, perhaps untranslatable word): "You kept God and did away with the Pope, when you should have done just the opposite." It was more than a quip. He had a real admiration for the Roman Church as an organization, though sometimes he would say it was like a school where the best students are always expelled.

He was simple in his tastes and manner of life; he worked for a living; he was completely unpretentious and deeply understanding; yet neither in his ideas nor his actions did he give evidence of any interest in social questions. Disorder and insecurity were distasteful to him, and he hated excess; this scorner of the lessons of history was in many ways a traditionalist. One day, at the family dinner table, he said in fun: "As for me, I'm a government anarchist." A mere boy dared retort to the Academician: "You're an anarchist because it's easy, and a conformist because it's safe." Tolerant with his family as with everyone, Paul Valéry smiled at this piece of impertinence. But it is quite true that conformity and anarchy combined in him in some strange way. An alert soldier, a scrupulous taxpayer, a punctilious civil servant, an indulgent father, he nevertheless was convinced that there is no such thing as a good government. Being acquainted with most of the politicians who governed France between the two world wars, he was on good terms with them as men, and even indignant at certain vicious attacks on them, but he had little respect for them as statesmen. The same boy mentioned above was once bombarding him with questions about what had been said at a luncheon attended by some of the prominent leaders of the time. Valéry answered impatiently: "What would you expect? Nothing of any interest. Anyway they don't know any more than anyone else. They are all buffoons."

These contrasting and even contradictory traits may explain how it was possible for the government and public alike to hold a mistaken notion of Valéry—a disservice to him insofar as it encouraged, in most people's minds, a misconception of the true direction of his thought; but on the other hand a service, since it allowed the Third Republic, not without a certain willful blindness, to make of him a sort of poet laureate: a member of the French Academy, a recipient of the highest decorations, a professor at the Collège de France, a spokesman for French culture abroad and in the League of Nations as well as on the more important state occasions at home. Some felt that he made the most of a mistake; actually nothing could have been more foreign to his nature. There was a great deal of candor in Valéry. It would have been nearer the truth to speak of his *adaptability*—compounded of skepticism, courtesy, real tolerance, and an innate finesse that probably came from his Italian blood.

The contrasting aspects of Valéry's character described above—they might well be taken for inconsistencies—became known only gradually in the course of his career. I can imagine that if, like so many others, he had been killed in the first World War (he was forty-four years old when it began, and had two children, so was not drafted), he would have been thought of as a rightist, not so very far from Charles Maurras or Albert Sorel in the political spectrum, though in fact he was poles apart from them. The works he had written up to that point (Valéry had *published* little before 1914, and nothing at all for the preceding fifteen years) would have brought him a reputation, all the greater perhaps for coming after his death, since the critics could then take the credit for discovering him. On several occasions in his youth he had taken an active interest in politics, but had lost it in later years. His views were typical of his generation, which had grown up in the decades after the defeat of 1871, in an atmosphere of constant threat from Bismarck's Germany. It was in this atmosphere that he wrote *Une Conquête métho-dique* (1897). Yet more revealing perhaps is the importance he attached to Japan's campaign against China (1895) and that of the United States against Spain (1898). These two events struck him as significant: "One was the first act of power by an Asiatic nation remodeled and equipped on European lines; the other was the first act of power against a European nation by a nation derived and, as it were, developed from Europe."

There is no doubt that the Dreyfus Affair played a part in this period of his life. It cooled his friendship with Marcel Schwob, and caused him to break with Kolbassine, a Russian friend he held in high regard. In that famous Affair, which drove all Frenchmen to take sides, why was he on the side of the nationalists? No doubt because he was, as I have just said, at heart a nationalist, and because, being so, he rejected the idea that the fate of one man, whatever his merit, could be weighed in the scales against the unity and efficacy of the State. It must not be forgotten that Valéry was at the time a young functionary in the War Ministry, that he was also still very much under the influence of the milieu in which he had grown up. Furthermore, he was exasperated with certain literary groups, most of them favorable to Dreyfus: it seemed to him that many of his friends were abusing their

role as intellectuals, in an affair which he believed had nothing
to do with ideas. His anti-Dreyfus sentiments were far from
platonic. It was the only time in his life that he ever came
close to being militant: he even signed an anti-Dreyfus mani-
festo and contributed to a fund for the widow of Colonel
Henry. The latter's suicide ought to have thrown some light
on the hidden aspects of the Affair and shown him that Dreyfus was innocent. But all minds were biased, even one so
acute as young Valéry's.

Such might well have been posterity's view of Paul Valéry's political opinions, if, instead of reacting to the event
of "war" by composing one of the most obscure poems in all
French literature—La Jeune Parque—he had been killed in
the fighting, in which he expected and hoped to take part.
But after the war, things changed. Valéry rose to fame with
extraordinary rapidity, though like Proust he had come to
public recognition late in life. In the light of what has just been
said of his part in the Dreyfus Affair, it is well to recall that
among those who first recognized his genius and helped to
make his reputation were a number of friends who were Jews.
As Valéry's thought gradually became known, he was seen to
be a rationalist deeply marked by nineteenth-century scientific ideas. He moved in milieus considered "progressive" at
the time: On Sundays at a friend's house in the Place du Pan-
théon, he would meet with Léon Blum, Paul Langevin, or
Jean Perrin; he talked on several occasions with Einstein. Being a "European" at a time when the European movement
was leftist—in opposition to the nationalists who hated the
Weimar Republic—Valéry lectured in Berlin (1926), with the
approval of Aristide Briand but to the displeasure of the rightists in the French Academy, to which he had just been elected.
Being a nonbeliever Valéry was considered a freemason—

which in France has a clear-cut political significance. He was violently attacked by the polemical rightists, and notably by the leader of the monarchists, Léon Daudet, whose aggressiveness may be accounted for by the fact that Valéry seemed, to those who did not care to look below the surface, to have made a political about-face.

The second World War found Valéry deeply pessimistic. For a Frenchman born under the defeat of 1871, the defeat of 1940 was a terrible blow. For the first time in his life his family saw him in tears. Having by chance been designated in 1931 to receive Marshal Pétain into the French Academy with the traditional eulogy, Valéry became his friend and, by forcing his pen perhaps, made of the Marshal the prototype of the warrior as a man of intellect. After the defeat, Valéry at first had confidence in Pétain, but very soon recognized that his regime was headed into an impasse. He was shocked by the revolting stupidity of the measures taken, particularly those affecting Jews and freemasons, and he intervened in behalf of several. In general, he reacted in much the same way as most Frenchmen, with the same ups and downs of opinion. During the hard winters of the German occupation, he listened like many others to the BBC—despite the jamming —and passionately followed on the map the advance of the Soviet and Allied armies. When he gave the funeral address for Bergson in 1941, he had deliberately and publicly contrasted the French philosopher's mind and character with German philosophy. After the liberation, he was disturbed by the peremptory punishment dealt out to some. If the victory brought him less joy than might have been expected, it was in part because he was already physically broken, and in part because he foresaw the difficulties and conflicts to come. He wanted the past forgotten: he wanted not so much to see

France rebuilt as to see her "built anew." But he saw that men and parties alike were making the same old mistakes, using the same old methods leading to the same disasters.

Although the works collected in the present volume were, most of them, dictated by some occasion or by chance, the reader will find that they group themselves around a few great themes: the death of civilizations, the relativity of history, the crisis of the mind, and the greatness and decline of Europe.

Valéry shows himself to be a penetrating and realistic observer. He had a premonition of some of the most decisive developments in the modern world, in certain cases long before they had fully evolved. After all, is there any other criterion for judging the value of a prognosis than the fact of its proving true in the event? The instability of modern civilizations, the profound revolution—almost a change of *phase*, in the physicist's sense—brought on by science and technology, the reaction on the mind itself, the transfer of international conflicts from the military to the economic plane, the repercussion of certain ideas spread by the West among less civilized nations—Paul Valéry not only sensed all this beforehand but described it with a foresight the more remarkable for being not so much a matter of intuition as an act of mind. He was simply applying in the political field a method of observation and analysis tested long and deeply on himself.

It is precisely by virtue of this fact that Paul Valéry's political writings—independently of their form, and even when history has caught up with them—have kept their vigor and actuality. The fact that Valéry had a premonition of Europe's troubles after the first and second World War; that he foresaw the rebirth of Asia, the awakening of the under-developed countries, the "cold war"; that his too often quoted "We later civilizations . . . we too now know that we are mortal" has found its full dramatic meaning in the atomic age; that now when man is taking leave of the earth, speed having made it too small, Valéry's dictum "The era of the finite world has begun" takes on a significance which only yesterday would have been unimaginable—all this indeed is worthy of note.

Yet far more interesting is another fact: that without relying directly or exclusively on any of the accepted methods of investigation—mathematics, statistics, economics, history, sociology, philosophy—Paul Valéry was able, generally, to reach the intellectual objectives he had set for himself at the very center of that disconcerting and contradictory reality before his eyes. Is it mere chance, then, that for Valéry—a solitary thinker in the dawn—thought had its economy, the intellect its strategy, and the mind its politics?

The remarkable thing is that Valéry's political thought is only, as it were, a by-product of his intense intellectual activity, turned generally more inward than outward. It was simply a matter of applying to a particular kind of problem the method he had developed to answer the needs of his solitary, obstinate, almost desperate intellectual enterprise, to which the mountain of notes accumulated in the course of fifty years bears witness.

Valéry excluded from his field of observation a whole series of topics ordinarily considered important. His thought developed in complete autonomy. He never hesitated to re-trace in his own way a path taken by others, even at the cost of seeming behind; but the way he chose was entirely his own, affording perspectives others had missed, and often leading further. Few men have had a truer sense of coming events, sometimes a half century before the fact.

In May, 1918, he wrote to André Gide: "Last night, re-read *Das Kapital*. . . . I am one of the few who have read it. This big book has remarkable things in it—you have only to find them. It's often short on logic, at times a desert of pedantry; but some of its analyses are marvelous. I mean that his method of getting at things is like the one I sometimes use, and I can frequently translate his language into mine."

Valéry and Marx: the parallel is not an obvious one. Who could be more a stranger to the pace and procedures of German philosophy than the Mediterranean Valéry? Besides, he said repeatedly—taking pride in the fact—that he was not a philosopher. For him, a system of metaphysics was simply a product of the mind like any other—like a poem, for instance. He pointedly noted that he had never read Hegel.

And yet, for Valéry a dialectic of the real did exist: Reality, as he conceived it, is composed of forces in a constantly shifting equilibrium; any given situation tends to produce its opposite. Such a constantly evolving reality sometimes undergoes actual mutations, involving even the mind itself. Indeed the milieu is inseparable from the observer, by virtue of their effect on each other. This is a strict relativism, in which there is no fixed or permanent system of reference. Valéry's dialectic has this peculiarity, that it has no metaphysical extension; it does not open out toward any absolute. The direction of his thought led him to an attitude that was primarily critical. This is the fundamental view in most of the essays of the present volume. But toward the end of his life, faced with the spectacle of world politics in the years just before the second World War, his views became far more radical.

He planned to draw up what he called the "Principles of Planned Anarchy." Just what he meant by the word "anarchy" he took the trouble to define: "Anarchy is the individual's effort to refuse obedience to any injunction the basis of which cannot be verified." In the rough draft he left among his papers, we see Valéry attacking every kind of myth, one after the other. The myth of politics: "The art of making people pay for, fight and torture one another for something they neither know nor care about." The myth of democracy: "The only meaning I can see in the word 'people' is 'mixture'; if you substitute for the word 'people' the words 'number' and 'mixture,' you will get some very odd terms . . . 'the sovereign mixture,' 'the will of the mixture,' etc." The economic myth: "An economy is not a society." The myth of political power: "No statesman ever measures up to his task, since the task is greater than any man's mind." The myth of the State: "You cannot attack one government without at the same time attacking all possible governments." And this remark, the force of which should not be underestimated: "We must have done with the fatal dogma of national sovereignty." His criticism was aimed at all parties. The Left: "The heart of the weak is hideous; anyone who suffers for a just cause or a creed has a poisonous serpent in his heart." The Center: "The middle groups are those who fear and hate to right and left of them." The Right: "The rightists have never had brains enough to pretend they have a heart." And here is an assault on all three: "Hatred, cruelty, hypocrisy, and graft belong to no single party, stupidity to no single regime, error to no single system. . . ."

Did they know what they were doing, on a beautiful day in July, 1945, in the presence of General de Gaulle—then head of the provisional government of the Republic—and of the highest authorities of the State, when they paid Paul Valéry the solemn tribute of a national funeral?

In demonstrating the bankruptcy of all politics, Valéry was not solely negative. He was much too realistic for that, and he had too much sense of responsibility. He simply believed that methods which had not changed since man's beginning could produce nothing good. It was not a matter of "Right" and "Left." The Right tends to keep what is of least value, whereas Revolution destroys with no thought of value, and often merely alters the terms of the problem. To Valéry's mind, there was no point in doing away with one myth merely to substitute another.

In fact, what Valéry set up in opposition to politics as such was *politics of the mind*. To the question "What should we want?" his answer was at once prudent and provisional, since no other could be objectively offered: "All politics," he said, "presuppose an idea of man." The idea of man, itself subject to periodic revision, can serve to orient political action if there are regular adjustments to keep pace with the progress of objective knowledge. Among his unpublished notes is this one, which I find significant: "Man is human only in small numbers; but these need the rest in order to carry on the incessant work of transformation and nonrepetition which distinguishes man from all that is nonhuman." It would be a mistake to give a Nietzschean interpretation to this remark; although, with the exception of Descartes, Nietzsche was the philosopher with whom Monsieur Teste had the closest affinity. The transformation Valéry had in mind was to work to the advantage of all, not of the few, by a constant exchange between the so-called masses and the so-called elite. The result would be to increase our intellectual capital—an ideal which, for Valéry, was more important than Justice, the latter, to his mind, being always "summary." He was allergic to the word "humanism," as he was to any word he thought vague and undefined; he detested it. Nevertheless, his whole thought was a kind of humanism, based not on traditional values but on what might be called *a reasonable use of reason*.

In certain respects, Valéry doubtless belonged to a great line of French rationalists—Descartes, Montesquieu, and Voltaire. It was in honor of Voltaire that he spoke on the last public occasion in which he took part. Like the eighteenth-century philosophers, he would probably have supported an enlightened despot, a man "in charge of the State," on the condition that he should put his power at the service of the Mind. Or perhaps, like Goethe, he wanted a sort of ideal Napoleon. Like Goethe, too, in witnessing the end of one century and the beginning of another, Paul Valéry lived through wars and changes of regime, not without anguish for his country and his family, but with serenity, obedient to duty and the conventions, accepting honors though not seeking them, and at the same time safeguarding his complete freedom for the exercise of his mind. Like Goethe again in his passion for the exact sciences, he tried his hand at every subject, from economics to strategy, from art criticism to medicine.

Something should be said of Valéry's style, which even the finest translation cannot wholly render. His prose, sometimes with almost too much magnificence, could clothe a naked thought and hide its subversive force. Yet to such showpieces one may prefer certain passages or raw fragments in which— the aridity of the subject notwithstanding—the prose writer is hardly distinct from the poet.

FRANÇOIS VALÉRY

Foreword

[1931]

THIS little collection* is dedicated above all to those persons who have no system and belong to no party and are therefore still free to doubt whatever is doubtful and to maintain what is not.

In any case, these are merely occasional studies. Some date from 1895, some from the recent past, some from the present. They have this characteristic in common—that they are essays, in the truest sense of the word. In them will be found little more than the intention of clarifying a few ideas that might really be called *political* if that fine word, so attractive and exciting to the mind, did not arouse great scruples and great repugnance in the mind of this author. He has wished merely to make a little clearer to himself the notions that he has received from others or that, like others, he has formed for himself—notions that everyone uses for thinking about human groups, their relations and difficulties with one another.

The effort to clarify such matters is assuredly not the business of those men who practice or mix in them. This book is the work of an amateur.

---

* This foreword was written for the first edition of *Regards sur le monde actuel* (1931), a much smaller collection than the present one.—J. M.

I do not know why the action by Japan against China and that of the United States against Spain, which followed the first quite closely, made a great impression on me at the time.* They were only limited conflicts in which forces of only moderate importance were engaged; and for myself I had no reason to be interested in such far-off things, since nothing in my ordinary occupations and concerns disposed me to be aware of them. And yet I felt these distinct events not as accidents or limited phenomena but as symptoms or premises, as significant facts whose meaning far exceeded their intrinsic importance and apparent scope. One was the first act of power by an Asiatic nation remodeled and equipped on European lines; the other was the first act of power against a European nation by a nation derived and, as it were, developed from Europe.

A shock that reaches us from an unforeseen quarter can give us a sudden, novel sensation of the existence of our body as an unknown quantity; we had been unaware of some part of what we were, and suddenly this brutal sensation makes us realize, by an aftereffect, the unsuspected size and shape of the field of our existence. Thus that indirect blow in the Far East and this direct blow in the West Indies made me dimly perceive something in myself that could be affected and troubled by such events. I found I was "sensitized" to situations that affected a kind of virtual idea of Europe which until then I had not known I held.

It had never occurred to me that *Europe* really existed. This name was to me no more than a geographical expression. It is only by chance that we are reminded of the permanent circumstances of our life; we perceive them only at the mo-

* 1895 and 1898. [P.V.]

4

ment when they suddenly alter. I shall take occasion later to show to what extent our unawareness of the simplest and most constant conditions of our existence and our judgments makes our conception of history so crude, our politics so inane and sometimes so naïve in its calculations. This unawareness leads even very great men to conceive schemes by imitation and to appraise them likewise, according to conventions whose inadequacy they do not realize.

In those days I had leisure to delve into the gaps in my mind. I began trying to develop my sense, my innate idea, of Europe. I called upon the little that I knew. I asked myself questions. I went back for a glance at certain books.

I imagined that it was necessary to study history and even to dig deeply into it in order to form a right idea of the present day. I knew that every mind preoccupied with the future of peoples was brought up on it. But for myself I could see in it only a *horrible confusion*. Under the heading of European history I found merely a collection of separate and parallel chronicles, tangled together at certain points. No *method* seemed to have anticipated the choice of "facts," decided upon their importance, or clearly determined the aim to be pursued. I noticed an incredible number of implicit hypotheses and ill-defined entities.

Since the subject of history is *the sum of those events or conditions which in the past may have come to the notice of some witness*, the methods of selecting, classifying, and expressing the facts that happen to have been preserved are not imposed on us by the nature of things. They ought to result from explicit analysis and decisions; but in practice they always give way to habits and traditional ways of thinking or speaking, whose accidental or arbitrary character we are unaware of. Nevertheless, we know that in all branches of knowledge decisive progress is made only at the moment when special notions, drawn from precise consideration of the objects of knowledge themselves and exactly fitted to connect that observation with the operations of thought and the latter with our powers of action, take the place of ordinary language—which is simply a means of crude approximation provided by education and usage. That vital moment when precise and specialized definitions and conventions replace meanings that are confused and statistical in origin has not yet arrived for history.

In fine, those books in which I sought the means to appreciate the curious effect on me of a few items of news, offered me a mere confusion of images, symbols, and theories from which I could deduce whatever I wanted, but not what I needed. Summing up my impressions, I said to myself that one kind of history aims at nothing more than painting a few scenes for us, on the understanding that such pictures are necessarily located in the "past." This convention has from the beginning produced very fine books; and among these there is no occasion to distinguish (since it is merely a matter of the pleasure or stimulus they provide) between those of real witnesses and those of imaginary witnesses. Such works are sometimes of an irresistible *truth*; they are like those portraits whose subjects have been dust for centuries and which still make us exclaim at the likeness. Nothing in the instantaneous effect on the reader enables him to distinguish, on the score of authenticity, between the tableaux of Tacitus, Michelet, Shakespeare, Saint-Simon, or Balzac. These men may all be considered creators, or all reporters, as you choose. The magic of the art of writing transports us in imagination into whatever epoch it pleases. That is why every gradation exists between pure story and pure history: historical fiction, fictional biography, etc. Moreover, we know that in history itself the supernatural sometimes appears. The personality of the reader is then directly brought into play, for it is his opinion that will admit or reject certain facts, decide what is history and what is not.

Another kind of history is composed of treatises so well constructed and reasoned, so sagacious, so rich in profound judgments on man and the evolution of affairs that we cannot imagine that things could have begun and developed in any other way.

Such works are marvels of the intellect. Some of them are surpassed by nothing else in literature or philosophy; but we must remember that the sentiments and colors with which the first kind charm and amuse us, and the admirable causality with which the second persuade us, come essentially from the talents of the writer and the critical resistance of the reader.

We might simply enjoy these fine fruits of the art of history, with no objection to their use, if politics were not wholly influenced by them. The *past*, being more or less imagined, or more or less organized after the event, acts on the future with a power comparable to that of the present itself. Sentiments and ambitions arise from memories of reading, from memories of memories, far more than they result from actual perceptions and data. What is truly characteristic of history is that it plays a part in history itself. The idea of the past takes on meaning and constitutes a value only for the man who has a passion for the future. The future, by definition, has no image. History provides us with the means to imagine it. History draws up for the imagination a table of situations and catastrophes, a gallery of ancestors, a formulary of acts, expressions, attitudes, and decisions, and presents them to our changeableness and uncertainty, to help us *to become*. When men or assemblies, faced with pressing or embarrassing circumstances, find themselves constrained to act, they do not in their deliberations consider the actual state of affairs *as something that has never occurred before*, but rather they consult their imaginary memories. Obeying a kind of law of *least action*, unwilling to create—that is, to answer the originality of the situation by invention—their hesitant thought tends toward automatism; it looks for precedents, yields to the spirit of history, which bids it first of all to *remember*, even when the case is an entirely new one. History feeds on history.

It is probable that Louis XVI would not have perished on the scaffold without the precedent of Charles I; that Bonaparte, if he had not meditated on the transformation of the Roman Republic into an empire founded on military power, would not have made himself emperor. He was passionately fond of reading history. All his life he dreamed of Hannibal, Caesar, Alexander, and Frederick the Great; and this man, born to create, who found himself in a position to reconstruct Europe politically—the climate of opinion being ready for it after three centuries of discovery and a revolutionary upheaval—lost himself among the perspectives of the past and the mirages of dead grandeur. The moment he ceased to astonish, he began to decline. He ruined himself by coming to resemble his adversaries, adoring their idols, imitating with all his might the thing that was their weakness, and substituting for his own direct vision of things the illusory décor of a policy based on history.

At the Congress of Berlin, Bismarck, dominated by the spirit of history which he mistook for the spirit of reality, would consider nothing but Europe, took no interest in

Africa, and used his genius and the prestige that made him master of the moment, solely to engage the Powers in colonial interests that would set them against each other, keep them rivals jealously divided, without foreseeing that the hour was at hand when Germany would ardently covet what she had provoked the other nations to share among themselves, thus allying them against herself who had come too late. He thought indeed of the morrow, but not of a morrow that had never before occurred.

Hand in hand with this overemphasis on someone else's more or less exact, more or less significant recollections, goes an absence or insufficiency of method in the choice, classification, and appraisal of the things recorded. In particular, history seems to take no account of the scale of the phenomena it presents. It fails to mention the relations that must necessarily exist between shape and size, in the events or situations it reports. And yet numbers and sizes are essential elements of description. It does not bother about problems of *similitude*. This is one of the reasons why the political use of history is so fallacious. What was possible within the space of an ancient city is no longer so within the dimensions of a great nation; what was true in the Europe of 1870 is no longer so when interests and connections extend over the whole earth. The very notions that we use for thinking and speaking of political objects, notions that have remained unchanged in spite of the prodigious change in the number and scope of relationships, have, without our noticing it, become deceptive or inapplicable. The word *people*, for example, had a precise meaning when it was possible to assemble *all* the citizens of a city about a mound, or in the Champ de Mars. But the increase in numbers, the passage from thousands to millions, has made of this word a monstrous term whose meaning depends on the sentence in which it occurs. Sometimes it describes the indistinct whole, never present anywhere; sometimes the majority as opposed to the limited number of richer or more cultivated individuals. . . .

The same observations apply to the passage of time. Nothing is easier than to point out in history books the omission of remarkable phenomena that have occurred so slowly as to be imperceptible. They escape the historian, since no document mentions them expressly. They could be perceived and noted only by means of a pre-established system of prior questions and definitions, which so far has never been conceived. An event that takes place over a century does not figure in any document or any collection of memoirs. For example, the immense and singular role of the city of Paris in the life of France after the Revolution. Or the discovery of electricity and the conquest of the earth by its different uses. The latter events, unequaled in human history, appear in it, when they do, less prominent than some other affair more *scenic*, more in conformity (this especially) with what traditional history customarily reports. In Napoleon's time electricity had about the same importance as Christianity at the time of Tiberius. It is gradually becoming obvious that this general *energizing* of the world is more pregnant with consequences, more capable of transforming life in the immediate future than all the "political" events from the time of Ampère to the present day.

It can be seen from these remarks how far our historical thought is dominated by unconscious traditions and conventions, how little it has been influenced by the universal revision and reorganization of every sphere of knowledge in modern times. Historical criticism has, of course, made great progress; but its role has been generally confined to discussing facts and establishing their probability; it is not interested in their quality. It accepts them and in its turn expresses them in conventional terms which, themselves, involve a whole tradition of concepts; and these introduce into history the basic disorder that comes from an endless number of observers or points of view. Every chapter of history contains a certain amount of subjective data and "arbitrary constants." The result is that the historian's problem is undefined once he goes beyond establishing or contesting the existence of some fact that may have come to the notice of some witness. The notion of an *event*, which is fundamental, seems not to have been reconsidered and re-thought as it should be, and this explains how relationships of the first importance have never been mentioned, or have not been sufficiently emphasized, as I shall show in a moment. Whereas in the natural sciences the accumulated experimentation of three hundred years has refashioned our way of seeing and has substituted for the observation and simple classification of objects whole systems of specially elaborated notions, yet in the historico-political field we are still at the stage of passive consideration and unsystematic observation. The same individual who in physics or biology uses forms of thought as accurate as precision instruments, thinks in politics by means of ambiguous terms, variable notions, illusory metaphors. The image of the world that takes shape and operates in political minds of various types and degrees is far from a satisfactory and methodical representation of the present.

Despairing of history, I began to think of the strange situation in which nearly all of us find ourselves—mere persons of good faith and good will, involved from birth in an inextricable politico-historical drama. Not one of us, by means of what he can observe in the sphere of his own experience, can put together and reconstruct the law of the political universe in which he finds himself. Even those who are best educated and best situated must think, as they recall what they know and compare it with what they see, that their knowledge only obscures the immediate political problem, which consists after all *in determining the relations of one man with the mass of men he does not know.* Anyone who is honest with himself and dislikes speculating on subjects that are not rationally related to his own experience, can hardly open his newspaper without plunging into a disorderly metaphysical world. What he reads, what he hears, curiously transcends what he observes or might observe. The sum of his impressions would be: *No politics without myths.*

So having closed all those books written in a language whose rules were obviously vague even for those who used it, I opened an atlas and abstractedly turned the pages of this portrait album of the world. I looked and pondered. First on the degree of accuracy of the maps I had before my eyes. I found in doing so a simple example of what, sixty years ago, was called *progress.* An old portolano, a map of the seventeenth century, and one of today: these three, I thought, clearly show its stages. . . .

A child's eye opens first on a chaos of lights and shadows, it turns and gets its bearings from moment to moment within a group of unequal intensities of light; and as yet there is nothing in common between the regions of light and the other sensations of his body. Meanwhile, the small movements of his body furnish him with a quite different mixture of impressions: he touches, pulls, presses; and within him is gradually formed a total awareness of his own shape. This knowledge is formulated out of distinct successive moments of sensation; the edifice of relationship and expectation is a product of contrasts and sequences. Sight, touch, and act are co-ordinated in a sort of multiple entry table, which is the tangible world, and finally—a capital *event*—it turns out that a certain system of correspondences is necessary and sufficient for a uniform adjustment of all the visual sensations to all the sensations of the skin and muscles. In the meantime, the child's *powers* are increasing and reality takes the form of an equilibrium in which the various sense impressions and the consequences of movement harmonize.

The human race has done precisely as the living child does when he wakens and develops in surroundings whose properties and extent he gradually explores and assembles by successive tries and connections. The species slowly and irregularly has come to recognize the shape of the earth's surface, has visited and depicted its parts more accurately, guessed at and verified its closed convexity, found and summed up the laws of its movement, discovered, appraised, exploited the resources and usable reserves of that thin layer in which all life is contained. . . .

Increased clarity and precision, and increased power: these are the essential facts of the history of modern times; and I consider them essential because they tend to modify man himself, and because the modification of life in its means of preservation, dissemination, and communication seems to me the criterion of importance that determines what facts are to be retained and pondered. This consideration transforms our judgments on history and politics, and reveals the gaps and disproportions, the arbitrary inclusions and omissions in them.

At this point in my reflections it appeared to me that the whole adventure of man up to our time should be divided into two very different phases, the first being comparable to that period of haphazard groping, of putting out and withdrawing feelers in formless surroundings, of bedazzlement, of sorties into the illimitable, which is the history of the child in the chaos of his first experiences. But then a certain order sets in; a new era begins. Actions in finite, well-determined, clearly delimited, abundantly and powerfully linked surroundings do not have the same characteristics or the same consequences as they had in a formless and undefined world.

It must be observed, however, that the two periods cannot be clearly distinguished in facts themselves. One fraction of mankind is already living in the second, while the rest still moves in the first. This disparity is the cause of a notable part of present-day complications.

Considering the whole of my epoch, then, and with the foregoing observations in mind, I tried to identify those circumstances which were the simplest and most general and at the same time were new.

What struck me at once was a considerable event, a fact of major importance, whose very importance, obviousness, and novelty, or rather singularity, had made it imperceptible to us, its contemporaries.

Every habitable part of the earth, in our time, has been discovered, surveyed, and divided up among nations. The era of unoccupied lands, open territories, places that belong to no one, hence the era of free expansion, has ended. There is no rock that does not bear a flag; there are no more blanks on the map; no region out of the reach of customs officials and the law; no tribe whose affairs do not fill some dossier and thus, under the evil spell of the written word, become the business of various well-meaning bureaucrats in their distant offices. *The age of the finite world has begun.* The general census of resources, the gathering of statistics on manpower, the development of media of communication are all under way. What could be more remarkable, more significant than taking the inventory, parceling out and linking together every part of the globe? The effects are already immense. An entirely new, excessive, and immediate interdependence between regions and events is the already perceptible consequence of this great fact. Henceforth we must see all political phenomena in the light of this new situation in the world; every one of them occurs either in obedience or in resistance to the effects of this definitive limitation and ever closer mutual dependence of human actions. The habits, ambitions, and loyalties formed in the course of earlier history do not cease to exist—but being insensibly transferred into quite differently constructed surroundings, they there lose their meaning and become causes of error and fruitless striving.

The total reconnaissance of the field of human life being now complete, the period of prospecting is giving way to a period of co-ordination. The parts of a finite, known world necessarily become more and more interlinked.

Hitherto, all politics gambled on the *isolation of events.* History was made up of events that could be *localized.* Any disturbance had, at one point on the globe as it were, a boundless medium in which to reverberate; its effects were nil at a sufficient distance; everything went on in Tokyo as though Berlin were at infinity. It was therefore possible—it was even reasonable—to predict, to calculate, and to act. There was room in the world for one or several great policies well planned and carried out.

That time is coming to an end. Henceforward every action will be re-echoed by many unforeseen interests on all sides; it will produce a chain of immediate events—confused reverberations in a closed space. The *effects of effects*, which were formerly imperceptible or negligible in relation to the length of a human life and to the radius of action of any human power, are now felt almost instantly at any distance; they return immediately to their causes, and only die away in the unpredictable. The expectations of the predictor are always disappointed, and that in a matter of months or a very few years.

In a few weeks, the most remote circumstances can change friend into foe, foe into ally, victory into defeat. No economic reasoning is possible. The greatest experts are wrong; paradox reigns.

There is no prudence, wisdom, or genius that is not quickly baffled by such complexity, for there is no more duration, continuity, or recognizable causality in this universe of multiple relations and contacts. Prudence, wisdom, and genius can be identified only by a series of successes; once accident and disorder are predominant, an expert or inspired game is in no way different from a game of chance; the finest gifts miscarry.

Hence the new politics are to the old what the short-term calculations of a stock market gambler—the nervous spurts of speculation on the floor of the exchange, the sudden fluctuations and reverses, the uncertain profits and losses—are to the old patriarchal economy, the slow, careful accumulation of a patrimony. . . . The long-pursued schemes and profound thought of a Machiavelli or a Richelieu would today have no more reliability and value than a "stock market tip."

This limited world, with the numerous and still multiplying links that hold it together, is also a world that is every day more highly equipped. Europe founded science, which has transformed life and vastly increased the power of those who possess it. But by its very nature science is essentially transmissible; it is necessarily reducible to universal methods and formulas. The means it affords to some, all can acquire.

But more than that, those means increase production, and not in quantity alone. To the traditional objects of commerce a host of new objects are added, and desire and need of them are spread by contagion or imitation. Soon the less advanced peoples are forced to acquire the knowledge necessary to appreciate and buy these new things, among which are the newest weapons. And the use of weapons against them, of course, drives them to procure weapons for themselves. They have no trouble in doing so; others fight to furnish them this equipment, and vie for the privilege of lending them the money to pay for it.

So the artificial imbalance of power on which European predominance has been based for three hundred years is tending rapidly to vanish. And another imbalance based on crude statistical characteristics tends to reappear.

Asia is about four times larger than Europe. The size of the American continent is slightly less than that of Asia. The population of China alone is at least equal to Europe's; Japan's is greater than Germany's.

Now, *local* European politics, dominating *general* European policy and making it absurd, has led rival Europeans to export the methods and the machines that made Europe supreme in the world. Europeans have competed for profit in awakening, instructing, and arming vast peoples who, before, were imprisoned in their traditions and asked nothing better than to remain so.

Just as the dissemination of culture among a people gradually makes the preservation of caste impossible, and as the possibility that commerce and industry can quickly make anyone rich has turned every kind of stable social hierarchy into an outworn illusion—so will it be with superiority based on technical power.

We shall eventually realize that there has been nothing more stupid in all history than European rivalry in matters of politics and economics, when compared, combined, and confronted with European unity and collaboration in matters of science. While the efforts of the best brains in Europe were amassing an immense capital of usable knowledge, the naïve tradition of a policy based on history, a policy of covetousness and ulterior motives, was being pursued; and the spirit of *Little Europe*, by a kind of treachery, handed over to the very people it meant to dominate, the methods and instruments of power. The competition for concessions or loans, for the purpose of sending out machines or experts, of establishing schools or arsenals—a competition that is nothing but the export far and wide of Western dissensions—is inevitably bringing about Europe's return to that secondary rank to which she is destined by her size, a rank from which the labors and internal exchanges of her intellect had lifted her. Europe will prove not to have had the politics worthy of her thought.

It is useless to imagine that violent events, gigantic wars, invasions *à la* Temuchin will be the result of our childish and disorderly behavior. All we need do is imagine the worst. Consider for a moment what will become of Europe when her own efforts have given to Asia two dozen Creusots or Essens, Manchesters or Roubaix, when steel, silk, paper, chemical products, fabrics, ceramics, and the rest are produced there in overwhelming quantities, at unbeatable prices, by the soberest and most numerous population in the world, its increase further favored by our introducing the practice of hygiene.

Such were my very simple reflections, with my atlas before me, when the two conflicts I mentioned and the requirements of a little study I was asked to make, at that time, of the methodical development of Germany, led me to these questions.

The great events that have since occurred have not caused me to modify these basic ideas, derived from quite simple and almost purely quantitative observations. "The Crisis of the Mind," which I wrote just after the peace, is hardly more than a development of these thoughts, which had come to me more than twenty years before. The immediate result of the Great War was what it was bound to be: it but accentuated and hastened the decadence of Europe. The simultaneous weakening of all her greatest nations; the glaring internal contradictions of principle; the despairing recourse of both sides to non-Europeans, very much like the recourse to foreigners during civil wars; the destruction of one another's prestige by Western nations in their war of propaganda; not to mention the accelerated spread of military methods and means, or the extermination of the elite: such were the consequences, for Europe's position in the world, of a crisis long prepared by so many illusions, and leaving behind it so many problems, puzzles, and fears—a situation more precarious, with minds more disturbed and the future darker than in 1913. In those days there was a balance of power in Europe; but today's peace can be thought of only as a kind of balance of weakness, necessarily more unstable.

THE OUTLOOK
FOR INTELLIGENCE

The Crisis of the Mind

[1919]

First Letter

WE LATER civilizations . . . we too now know that we are mortal.

We had long heard tell of whole worlds that had vanished, of empires sunk without a trace, gone down with all their men and all their machines into the unexplorable depths of the centuries, with their gods and their laws, their academies and their sciences pure and applied, their grammars and their dictionaries, their Classics, their Romantics, and their Symbolists, their critics and the critics of their critics. . . . We were aware that the visible earth is made of ashes, and that ashes signify something. Through the obscure depths of history we could make out the phantoms of great ships laden with riches and intellect; we could not count them. But the disasters that had sent them down were, after all, none of our affair.

Elam, Nineveh, Babylon were but beautiful vague names, and the total ruin of those worlds had as little significance for us as their very existence. But France, England, Russia . . . these too would be beautiful names. *Lusitania*, too, is a beautiful name. And we see now that the abyss of history is deep enough to hold us all. We are aware that a civilization has the same fragility as a life. The circumstances that could send the works of Keats and Baudelaire to join the works of Menander are no longer inconceivable; they are in the newspapers.

23

That is not all. The searing lesson is more complete still. It was not enough for our generation to learn from its own experience how the most beautiful things and the most ancient, the most formidable and the best ordered, can perish *by accident*; in the realm of thought, feeling, and common sense, we witnessed extraordinary phenomena: paradox suddenly become fact, and obvious fact brutally belied.

I shall cite but one example: the great virtues of the German peoples have begotten more evils, than idleness ever bred vices. With our own eyes, we have seen conscientious labor, the most solid learning, the most serious discipline and application adapted to appalling ends.

So many horrors could not have been possible without so many virtues. Doubtless, much science was needed to kill so many, to waste so much property, annihilate so many cities in so short a time; but *moral qualities* in like number were also needed. Are Knowledge and Duty, then, suspect?

So the Persepolis of the spirit is no less ravaged than the Susa of material fact. Everything has not been lost, but everything has sensed that it might perish.

An extraordinary shudder ran through the marrow of Europe. She felt in every nucleus of her mind that she was no longer the same, that she was no longer herself, that she was about to lose consciousness, a consciousness acquired through centuries of bearable calamities, by thousands of men of the first rank, from innumerable geographical, ethnic, and historical coincidences.

So—as though in desperate defense of her own physiological being and resources—all her memory confusedly returned. Her great men and her great books came back pell-mell. Never has so much been read, nor with such passion, as during the war: ask the booksellers. . . . Never have people prayed so much and so deeply: ask the priests. All the saviors, founders, protectors, martyrs, heroes, all the fathers of their country, the sacred heroines, the national poets were invoked. . . .

And in the same disorder of mind, at the summons of the same anguish, all cultivated Europe underwent the rapid revival of her innumerable ways of thought: dogmas, philosophies, heterogeneous ideals; the three hundred ways of explaining the World, the thousand and one versions of Christianity, the two dozen kinds of positivism; the whole spectrum of intellectual light spread out its incompatible colors, illuminating with a strange and contradictory glow the death agony of the European soul. While inventors were feverishly searching their imaginations and the annals of former wars for the means of doing away with barbed wire, of outwitting submarines or paralyzing the flight of airplanes, her soul was intoning at the same time all the incantations it ever knew, and giving serious consideration to the most bizarre prophecies; she sought refuge, guidance, consolation throughout the whole register of her memories, past acts, and ancestral attitudes. Such are the known effects of anxiety, the disordered behavior of a mind fleeing from reality to nightmare and from nightmare back to reality, terrified, like a rat caught in a trap. . . .

The military crisis may be over. The economic crisis is still with us in all its force. But the intellectual crisis, being more subtle and, by its nature, assuming the most deceptive appearances (since it takes place in the very realm of dissimulation) . . . this crisis will hardly allow us to grasp its true extent, its *phase*.

No one can say what will be dead or alive tomorrow, in

literature, philosophy, aesthetics; no one yet knows what ideas and modes of expression will be inscribed on the casualty list, what novelties will be proclaimed.

Hope, of course, remains—singing in an undertone:

> *Et cum vorandi vicerit libidinem*
> *Late triumphet imperator spiritus.*

But hope is only man's mistrust of the clear foresight of his mind. Hope suggests that any conclusion unfavorable to us *must be* an error of the mind. And yet the facts are clear and pitiless: thousands of young writers and young artists have died; the illusion of a European culture has been lost, and knowledge has been proved impotent to save anything whatever; science is mortally wounded in its moral ambitions and, as it were, put to shame by the cruelty of its applications; idealism is barely surviving, deeply stricken, and called to account for its dreams; realism is hopeless, beaten, routed by its own crimes and errors; greed and abstinence are equally flouted; faiths are confused in their aim—cross against cross, crescent against crescent; and even the skeptics, confounded by the sudden, violent, and moving events that play with our minds as a cat with a mouse . . . even the skeptics lose their doubts, recover, and lose them again, no longer master of the motions of their thought.

The swaying of the ship has been so violent that the best-hung lamps have finally overturned. . . .

What gives this critical condition of the mind its depth and gravity is the patient's condition when she was overcome.

I have neither the time nor the ability to define the intellectual situation in Europe in 1914. And who could pretend to picture that situation? The subject is immense, requiring

26

every order of knowledge and endless information. Besides, when such a complex whole is in question, the difficulty of reconstructing the past, even the recent past, is altogether comparable to that of constructing the future, even the near future; or rather, they are the same difficulty. The prophet is in the same boat as the historian. Let us leave them there.

For all I need is a vague general recollection of what was being thought just before the war, the kinds of intellectual pursuit then in progress, the works being published.

So if I disregard all detail and confine myself to a quick impression, to that *natural whole* given by a moment's perception, I see ... *nothing*! Nothing ... and yet an infinitely potential nothing.

The physicists tell us that if the eye could survive in an oven fired to the point of incandescence, it would see ... nothing. There would be no unequal intensities of light left to mark off points in space. That formidable contained energy would produce invisibility, indistinct equality. Now, equality of that kind is nothing else than a perfect state of *disorder*.

And what made that disorder in the mind of Europe? The free coexistence, in all her cultivated minds, of the most dissimilar ideas, the most contradictory principles of life and learning. That is characteristic of a *modern* epoch.

I am not averse to generalizing the notion of "modern" to designate a certain way of life, rather than making it purely a synonym of *contemporary*. There are moments and places in history to which *we moderns* could return without too greatly disturbing the harmony of those times, without seeming objects infinitely curious and conspicuous ... creatures shocking, dissonant, and unassimilable. Wherever our entrance would create the least possible sensation, that is where we should feel almost at home. It is clear that Rome in the time of Trajan, or Alexandria under the Ptolemies, would take us in more easily than many places less remote in time but more specialized in a single type of manners and entirely given over to a single race, a single culture, and a single system of life.

Well then! Europe in 1914 had perhaps reached the limit of modernism in this sense. Every mind of any scope was a crossroads for all shades of opinion; every thinker was an international exposition of thought. There were works of the mind in which the wealth of contrasts and contradictory tendencies was like the insane displays of light in the capitals of those days: eyes were fatigued, scorched. . . . How much material wealth, how much labor and planning it took, how many centuries were ransacked, how many heterogeneous lives were combined, to make possible such a carnival, and to set it up as the supreme wisdom and the triumph of humanity?

In a book of that era—and not one of the most mediocre—we should have no trouble in finding: the influence of the Russian ballet, a touch of Pascal's gloom, numerous impressions of the Goncourt type, something of Nietzsche, something of Rimbaud, certain effects due to a familiarity with painters, and sometimes the tone of a scientific publication . . . the whole flavored with an indefinably British quality difficult to assess! . . . Let us notice, by the way, that within each of the components of this mixture other *bodies* could well be found. It would be useless to point them out: it would be merely to repeat what I have just said about modernism, and to give the whole history of the European mind.

Standing, now, on an immense sort of terrace of Elsinore that stretches from Basel to Cologne, bordered by the sands of

Nieuport, the marshes of the Somme, the limestone of Champagne, the granites of Alsace . . . our Hamlet of Europe is watching millions of ghosts.

But he is an intellectual Hamlet, meditating on the life and death of truths; for ghosts, he has all the subjects of our controversies; for remorse, all the titles of our fame. He is bowed under the weight of all the discoveries and varieties of knowledge, incapable of resuming this endless activity; he broods on the tedium of rehearsing the past and the folly of always trying to innovate. He staggers between two abysses— for two dangers never cease threatening the world: order and disorder.

Every skull he picks up is an illustrious skull. *Whose was it?** This one was *Lionardo*. He invented the flying man, but the flying man has not exactly served his inventor's purposes. We know that, mounted on his great swan (*il grande uccello sopra del dosso del suo magnio cecero*) he has other tasks in our day than fetching snow from the mountain peaks during the hot season to scatter it on the streets of towns. And that other skull was *Leibnitz*, who dreamed of universal peace. And this one was *Kant* . . . *and Kant begat Hegel, and Hegel begat Marx, and Marx begat. . . .*

Hamlet hardly knows what to make of so many skulls. But suppose he forgets them! Will he still be himself? . . . His terribly lucid mind contemplates the passage from war to peace: darker, more dangerous than the passage from peace to war; all peoples are troubled by it. . . . "What about Me," he says, "what is to become of Me, the European intellect?. . . And what is peace? . . . *Peace is perhaps that state of things in which the natural hostility between men is manifested in creation, rather than destruction as in war.* Peace is a time of creative

*Hamlet's words are in English in the French text.—J.M.

rivalry and the battle of production; but am I not tired of producing? . . . Have I not exhausted my desire for radical experiment, indulged too much in cunning compounds? . . . Should I not perhaps lay aside my hard duties and transcendent ambitions? . . . Perhaps follow the trend and do like Polonius who is now director of a great newspaper; like Laertes, who is something in aviation; like Rosencrantz, who is doing God knows what under a Russian name?

"Farewell, ghosts! The world no longer needs you—or me. By giving the name of progress to its own tendency to a fatal precision, the world is seeking to add to the benefits of life the advantages of death. A certain confusion still reigns; but in a little while all will be made clear, and we shall witness at last the miracle of an animal society, the perfect and ultimate anthill."

Second Letter

I was saying the other day that peace is the kind of war that allows acts of love and creation in its course; it is, then, a more complex and obscure process than war properly so-called, as life is more obscure and more profound than death.

But the origin and early stages of peace are more obscure than peace itself, as the fecundation and beginnings of life are more mysterious than the functioning of a body once it is made and adapted.

Everyone today feels the presence of this mystery as an actual sensation; a few men must doubtless feel that their own inner being is positively a part of the mystery; and perhaps there is someone with a sensibility so clear, subtle, and rich that he senses in himself certain aspects of our destiny more advanced than our destiny itself.

I have not that ambition. The things of the world interest

me only as they relate to the intellect; for me, everything relates to the intellect. Bacon would say that this notion of the intellect is an *idol*. I agree, but I have not found a better idol.

I am thinking then of the establishment of peace insofar as it involves the intellect and things of the intellect. This point of view is *false*, since it separates the mind from all other activities; but such abstract operations and falsifications are inevitable: every point of view is false.

A first thought dawns. The idea of culture, of intelligence, of great works, has for us a very ancient connection with the idea of Europe—so ancient that we rarely go back so far.

Other parts of the world have had admirable civilizations, poets of the first order, builders, and even scientists. But no part of the world has possessed this singular *physical* property: the most intense power of radiation combined with an equally intense power of assimilation.

Everything came to Europe, and everything came from it. Or almost everything.

Now, the present day brings with it this important question: can Europe hold its pre-eminence in all fields?

Will Europe become *what it is in reality*—that is, a little promontory on the continent of Asia?

Or will it remain *what it seems*—that is, the elect portion of the terrestrial globe, the pearl of the sphere, the brain of a vast body?

In order to make clear the strict necessity of this alternative, let me develop here a kind of basic theorem.

Consider a map of the world. On this planisphere are all the habitable lands. The whole is divided into regions, and in each of these regions there is a certain density of population, a certain quality of men. In each of these regions, also, there are corresponding natural resources—a more or less fertile soil, a more or less rich substratum, a more or less watered terrain, which may be more or less easily developed for transport, etc.

All these characteristics make it possible, at any period, to classify the regions we are speaking of, so that at any given time *the situation on the earth may be defined by a formula showing the inequalities between the inhabited regions of its surface*.

At each moment, the *history* of the next moment will depend on this given inequality.

Let us now examine, not our theoretical classification, but the one that actually prevailed in the world until recently. We notice a striking fact, which we take too much for granted:

Small though it be, Europe has for centuries figured at the head of the list. In spite of her limited extent—and although the richness of her soil is not out of the ordinary—she dominates the picture. By what miracle? Certainly the miracle must lie in the high quality of her population. That quality must compensate for the smaller number of men, of square miles, of tons of ore, found in Europe. In one scale put the empire of India and in the other the United Kingdom: the scale with the smaller weight tilts down!

That is an extraordinary upset in equilibrium. But its consequences are still more so: *they will shortly allow us to foresee a gradual change in the opposite direction*.

We suggested just now that the quality of her men must be the determining factor in Europe's superiority. I cannot analyze this quality in detail; but from a summary examination I would say that a driving thirst, an ardent and disinterested curiosity, a happy mixture of imagination and rigorous logic, a certain unpessimistic skepticism, an unresigned mysticism . . . are the most specifically active characteristics of the European psyche.

A single example of that spirit, an example of the highest order and of the very first importance, is Greece—since the whole Mediterranean littoral must be counted in Europe. Smyrna and Alexandria are as much a part of Europe as Athens and Marseilles. Greece founded geometry. It was a mad undertaking: we are still arguing about the *possibility* of such a folly.

What did it take to bring about that fantastic creation? Consider that neither the Egyptians nor the Chinese nor the Chaldeans nor the Hindus managed it. Consider what a fascinating adventure it was, a conquest a thousand times richer and actually far more poetic than that of the Golden Fleece. No sheepskin is worth the golden thigh of Pythagoras.

This was an enterprise requiring gifts that, when found together, are usually the most incompatible. It required argonauts of the mind, tough pilots who refused to be either lost in their thoughts or distracted by their impressions. Neither the frailty of the premises that supported them, nor the infinite number and subtlety of the inferences they explored could dismay them. They were as though equidistant from the inconsistent Negro and the indefinite fakir. They accomplished the extremely delicate and improbable feat of adapting common speech to precise reasoning; they analyzed the most complex combinations of motor and visual functions, and found that these corresponded to certain linguistic and grammatical properties; they trusted in words to lead them through space like far-seeing blind men. And space itself became, from century to century, a richer and more surprising creation, as thought gained possession of itself and had more confidence in the marvelous system of reason and in the original intuition which had endowed it with such incomparable instruments as definitions, axioms, lemmas, theorems, problems, porisms, etc.

I should need a whole book to treat the subject properly. I wanted merely to indicate in a few words one of the characteristic inventions of the European genius. This example brings me straight back to my thesis.

I have claimed that the imbalance maintained for so long in Europe's favor was, *by its own reaction*, bound to change by degrees into an imbalance in the opposite direction. That is what I called by the ambitious name of basic theorem.

How is this proposition to be proved? I take the same example, that of the geometry of the Greeks; and I ask the reader to consider the consequences of this discipline through the ages. We see it gradually, very slowly but very surely, assuming such authority that all research, all the ways of acquiring knowledge tend inevitably to borrow its rigorous procedure, its scrupulous economy of "matter," its automatic generalizations, its subtle methods, and that infinite discretion which authorizes the wildest audacity. Modern science was born of this education in the grand style.

But once born, once tested and proved by its practical applications, our science became a means of power, a means of physical domination, a creator of material wealth, an apparatus for exploiting the resources of the whole planet—ceasing to be an "end in itself" and an artistic activity. Knowledge, which was a consumer value, became an exchange value. The utility of knowledge made knowledge a *commodity*, no longer desired by a few distinguished amateurs but by Everybody.

This commodity, then, was to be turned out in more and

more manageable or consumable forms; it was to be distributed to a more and more numerous clientele; it was to become
an article of commerce, an article, in short, that can be imi-
tated and produced almost anywhere.

Result: the inequality that once existed between the regions of the world as regards the mechanical arts, the applied
sciences, the scientific instruments of war or peace—an inequality on which Europe's predominance was based—is
tending gradually to disappear.

So, the classification of the habitable regions of the world is
becoming one in which gross material size, mere statistics and
figures (e.g., population, area, raw materials) finally and alone
determine the rating of the various sections of the globe.

And so the scales that used to tip in our favor, although
we *appeared* the lighter, are beginning to lift us gently, as
though we had stupidly shifted to the other side the mysterious
excess that was ours. *We have foolishly made force proportional*
to mass!

This coming phenomenon, moreover, may be connected
with another to be found in every nation: I mean the diffusion of culture, and its acquisition by ever larger categories
of individuals.

An attempt to predict the consequences of such diffusion,
or to find whether it will or not inevitably bring on *decadence*,
would be a delightfully complicated problem in intellectual
physics.

The charm of the problem for the speculative mind proceeds, first, from its *resemblance* to the physical fact of diffusion and, next, from a sudden transformation into a profound
difference when the thinker remembers that his primary object is *men* not *molecules*.

35

A drop of wine falling into water barely colors it, and tends to disappear after showing as a pink cloud. That is the physical fact. But suppose now that some time after it has vanished, gone back to limpidity, we should see, here and there in our glass—which seemed once more to hold *pure* water—drops of wine forming, dark and *pure*—what a surprise! . . .

This phenomenon of Cana is not impossible in intellectual and social physics. We then speak of *genius*, and contrast it with diffusion.

Just now we were considering a curious balance that worked in inverse ratio to weight. Then we saw a liquid system pass as though spontaneously from homogeneous to heterogeneous, from intimate mingling to clear separation. . . . These paradoxical images give the simplest and most practical notion of the role played in the World by what—for five or ten thousand years—has been called Mind.

But can the European Mind—or at least its most precious content—be totally diffused? Must such phenomena as democracy, the exploitation of the globe, and the general spread of technology, all of which presage a *deminutio capitis* for Europe . . . must these be taken as absolute decisions of fate? Or have we some freedom *against* this threatening conspiracy of things?

Perhaps in seeking that freedom we may create it. But in order to seek it, we must for a time give up considering groups, and study the thinking individual in his struggle for a personal life against his life in society.

A Fond Note on Myth

[1928]

A LADY, my dear . . . a quite unknown lady has written me a very long and rather tender letter, asking me many difficult questions on which she affects to think that I can relieve her mind.

She is worried about my attitude toward God and love, whether I have faith in both; she would like to know if pure poetry is fatal to feeling, and asks me if I practice analyzing my dreams as is done in Central Europe, where no right-thinking person fails to fish up out of his own depths every morning some abysmal enormity, some obscenely shaped octopus he is proud to have fostered.

On these and several other doubts, I was able to enlighten or reassure her without serious trouble. I am no great light, but little is needed on great subjects. Besides, the tone is everything: a certain elegance appeases, a certain turn of speech uplifts, certain graces beguile the tender soul with pleasure as she reads, not so much asking to be answered—for that would put an end to the game and take the life out of the pretext—as to be, herself, questioned.

However, I felt quite baffled by one precise and very particular problem, one of those that cannot be got rid of without a great deal of reading and reflection.

Reading is tedious for me; hardly anything, except per-

37

haps writing, tries my patience more. I am good only at inventing what I need at the moment. I am a wretched Crusoe on an island of flesh and mind entirely surrounded by ignorance, having crudely created my own tools and my own arts. I sometimes congratulate myself on being so poor and so incapable of the treasures of accumulated knowledge. I am poor, but a king; and doubtless, like Crusoe, I reign over nothing but my own inner monkeys and parrots; but that is to reign nonetheless. . . . I believe, indeed, that our ancestors read too much and that our brains are a gray pulp squeezed from books. . . .

I now come back to my questioner, whom I left suspended for a moment on some nail of time. This woman, whose face I have never seen, of whom I know nothing but the scent of her writing paper (a powerful scent that gives me a notion of nausea), shows an astonishing insistence in trying to make me explain myths and the science of myth, which she wants me at all costs to discuss and about which I know only what I choose. I cannot guess what they can mean to her.

If only it had been you, my wise and simple friend, and your curiosity on this point had tried to stir my laziness, you would never have got anything out of my head but sheer banter, most of it impure and the rest frivolous. Between people who know each other only in spirit—as is the case with you and me, alas!—nothing counts except that mysterious accord between their natures; words do not count, acts are nothing. . . .

And so, my dearest familiar, since I went so far as to reply to that perfumed absence—and God knows why I answered her, what obscure hopes, what hints of sweet risk seduced me into writing to her—I shall pass on to you the substance of what I imagined for her sake. I had to feign a knowledge I do not have and do not envy in those who have it. Happy are the possessors thereof! But however solid it may be, unhappy are those who rely on it!

I must first confess to you that when I set about conceiving the world of myth, my mind balked; I urged it on, prodding its boredom and resistance; and as it recoiled under my pressure, glancing backward at what it loves, longing for what it can do best, and depicting for me only too vividly all such attractions, I furiously drove it in among the monsters, into all that melee of gods, demons, heroes, and horrible works of nature, all those creatures of the ancients, who set their philosophy as ardently to peopling the universe as we were later to set ours to emptying it of all life. In their darkness, our ancestors coupled with every enigma and begat strange children.

I was at a loss which way to turn in that chaos of mine, what to fasten on as my beginning, so as to develop the vague thoughts which that tumult of images and memories, numberless names, and confused conjectures at once awoke and dismissed in me as I set about my task.

My pen jabbed the paper, my left hand tortured my face, my eyes perceived too clearly some well-lit object, and I felt only too strongly that I had no call to write. Then my pen, which was killing time in little strokes, began of itself to sketch baroque shapes, hideous fish, octopuses in a tousle of all too fluent and easy flourishes. . . . It was creating *myths*; they flowed from my expectant self, while my mind, hardly seeing what my hand was inventing right before it, wandered like a sleepwalker among the dark imaginary walls and submarine theaters of the aquarium at Monaco!

Who knows, I thought, whether the real in its numberless forms is not as arbitrary, as gratuitously produced as these animals in arabesque? When I dream and invent without a backward glance, am I not . . . Nature? Provided the pen touches the paper and is full of ink, and I am bored and abstracted . . . I create! A random word coming to mind has an endless destiny, grows organs of phrase, and one phrase requires another, which may have existed before it; it desires a past, to which it gives birth in order to be born itself . . . after it is already in existence! And these curves, these convolutions, these tentacles, feelers, feet, and appendages which I spin out over the page . . . does not Nature in her own way do the same, in play, when she pours out, transforms, spoils, forgets, and rediscovers so many chances and shapes of life among the rays and atoms, where the possible and the inconceivable are teeming and entangled?

The mind sets about it in just the same way. But it goes one better than Nature; not only does it create, as she does, but on top of that it *appears* to create. It joins the lie to truth; and whereas life or reality confines itself to proliferating within the instant, the mind has spun for itself the myth of myths, the undefined element of all myth—which is *Time*. . . .

But time and the lie could not exist without some sort of artifice. Speech is the means required for multiplying in the void.

And here is how I finally came round to my subject and evolved a theory for that soulful but invisible lady.

Lady, I said to her, O myth! *Myth* is the name of everything that exists and abides with speech as its only cause. There is no discourse so obscure, no tale so odd or remark so incoherent that it cannot be given a meaning. There is always some supposition to give a meaning even to the strangest language.

Just imagine that several accounts of the same affair, or

diverse reports of the same event, are given to you in books or by witnesses who do not agree among themselves, though all are equally trustworthy. To say that they do not agree is to say that their simultaneous diversity makes up a monster. Their rivalry gives birth to a chimera. . . . But a monster or a chimera, though not viable in reality, is at ease in the vagueness of people's minds. A combination of woman and fish is a mermaid, and the form of a mermaid is easily accepted. But is a living mermaid possible?—I am not at all sure that we are yet so expert in the sciences of life that we can refuse life to mermaids by demonstrative reasoning. Much anatomy and physiology would be needed to find anything against them except this fact: modern man has never fished one up!

Whatever perishes from a little more clarity is a myth. Under the rigorous eye, under the repeated and convergent blows of questions and categories with which the alert mind is armed at all points, myths die and the fauna of vague things and vague ideas wither away. . . . Myths decompose in the light within us made up of the combined presence of our body and the utmost degree of consciousness.

See how a nightmare weaves a powerful drama from the various independent sensations working on us in our sleep. The hand is caught under the body; an uncovered foot, free from the bedclothes, cools at a distance from the rest of the sleeper; early morning passers-by shout in the street at dawn; the empty stomach stretches and yawns, the entrails rumble; a ray from the great rising sun vaguely disturbs the retina through the closed eyelids. . . . All these are separate and incoherent facts; and there is *no one as yet* to reduce them to what they are and to the known world, to organize them, retain some and discard others, decide their values, and allow us to go beyond them. But together they are all, as it were, equal conditions and must be equally satisfied. The result is an original and absurd creation, incompatible with the rest of life, all-powerful and most frightening, *having within itself no means of terminating, no issue, no limit.* . . . The same is true of the details of our waking life, but with less unity. The whole history of thought is nothing but the play of an infinite number of small nightmares of great consequence, whereas in sleep we have great nightmares of very short, very slight consequence.

All our language is composed of brief little dreams; and the wonderful thing is that we sometimes make of them strangely accurate and marvelously reasonable thoughts.

In truth, there are so many myths in us, they are so familiar a part of us, that it is almost impossible to pick out clearly in our minds anything that is not a myth. We cannot even speak of them without mythifying, and am I not at this moment creating a myth about myth, in reply to the caprice of a myth?

No, my dear familiars, I can find no way of escape from what is not! Speech so fills us, fills everything with its images that we cannot think how to begin to refrain from imagining —nothing is without it. . . .

Remember that tomorrow is a myth, that the universe is one; that numbers, love, the real, and the infinite . . . that justice, the people, poetry . . . the earth itself are myths! And even the pole is one, for those who claim to have been there thought they were there only for reasons that are inseparable from speech. . . .

I forgot to mention the whole of the past. . . . All history is made up of nothing but thoughts to which we attribute the essentially mythical value of representing what was. Each instant falls at each instant into the imaginary, and we are hardly dead before we are off, with the speed of light, to join the centaurs and the angels. . . . But that is putting it mildly! Hardly are our backs turned, hardly are we out of sight, before opinion makes of us whatever it can!

To come back to history. See how imperceptibly it changes into dream as it gets farther from the present! Near us, its myths are still temperate, restrained by not unbelievable documents, material traces that somewhat moderate our fancy. But once beyond three or four thousand years before our birth, we are quite at liberty. And finally, in the void of the myth of pure time, innocent of anything at all resembling what is around us, the mind—sure only that there was *something*, and forced by its own necessity to presuppose antecedents and "causes" as supports for what is, or for what *it* is— gives birth to epochs, states, events, people, principles, images, or stories more and more naïve, reminding us of (or amounting to no more than) that candid cosmology of the Hindus, when, in order to support the earth in space, they situated it on the back of an immense elephant; this beast stood on a tortoise; which, in turn, was borne up by a sea contained in who knows what container. . . .

The profoundest philosopher, the best-trained physicist, the geometrician best equipped with those means which Laplace grandly called "the resources of the most sublime analysis". . . cannot, and knows not how to do otherwise.

That is why one day I happened to write: "In the beginning was the Fable!"

Which means that every origin, every dawn of things is of the same substance as the songs and tales around a cradle. . . .

It is a kind of absolute law that everywhere, in every place and every period of civilization, in every belief, in every discipline and every relationship . . . the false supports the true; the true takes the false as its ancestor, its cause, its author, its origin and end, without exception or remedy—and the true engenders the false, from which in turn it requires to be engendered. All antiquity, all causality, all principles of things are fabulous inventions and obey simple laws.

What should we be without the help of that which does not exist? Very little. And our unoccupied minds would languish if fables, mistaken notions, abstractions, beliefs, and monsters, hypotheses and the so-called problems of metaphysics did not people with beings and objectless images our natural depths and darkness.

Myths are the souls of our actions and our loves. We cannot act without moving toward a phantom. We can love only what we create.

That, my dear, was nearly the whole of my discourse to that bodiless woman who may, I fear—though it doesn't displease me—have made you jealous. I will spare you a few phrases in the grand style with which I thought it necessary to round off such remarks.

I even put a little poetry into the last few moments of my letter. A lady cannot be left a prey to naked notions; goodbys must be gilded. So I allowed myself to say to my unknown lady that both the dawn and the evening of time, like those of a beautiful day enchanted and illumined by the magic of the sun setting beyond the horizon, are painted and peopled with miracles. Just as the almost level light creates prodigious pleasures for the human eye, gorging it with magic, with ideal transmutations, enormous forms borne up elaborately in the heavens, shapes of other worlds, blazing abodes with golden rocks, the purest of lakes, thrones, wandering grottoes, superb hells, scenes of faërie; just, too, as those dazzling summits, those phantasms, monsters, and aerial deities dissolve into vapor and decomposing rays . . . so it is with all the gods and all our idols, even the abstract ones: what was, what will be, all that happens far away. Whatever our mind wants, the origins it seeks, the results and solutions it thirsts after, all these it cannot help deriving from itself, suffering them in itself. Cut off from experience, isolated from the constraints imposed by direct contact, the mind engenders what it needs, in its own fashion.

It withdraws into itself and utters the extraordinary. From its slightest accidents it spouts supernatural creations. In this state, it uses everything it is; a mistake, a misunderstanding, a pun can fertilize it. It gives the name of science and art to its power of conferring upon its own phantasmagoria a clarity, a duration, a consistency, and even a rigor astonishing to itself—sometimes even overwhelming!

Good-by, my dear; I was just coming back to the subject of love.

A Conquest by Method

[1897]

Prefatory Note (1934)

It was around 1895 that England began to be no longer insensitive to the pressure of German power at the essential points of her economic life and her empire.

She had not been aware, until then, that she was threatened in the exercise of her vital functions by an eleventh-hour rival, as ill situated on the map as in time. Tarde venientibus ossa, *she would have said, if she had said anything.*

But to be an island, to have coal, political and maritime traditions, a simple and indomitable will, an immense clientele directly or indirectly subjugated, an imposing self-assurance in desires and designs, is not everything. Security brings with it a kind of inertia. The English mind never hesitates to alter what seems bad, *but it can for a long time resist changing what was once* good *and still satisfies it. This trait of the English character is perhaps due to its habitual certainty, hitherto always confirmed by history, that there will be ample time to see and repel any danger, thanks to the sea moat and to the fleet watching it.*

But in an era permeated by the sciences—an era constantly in a state of technical transformation, and in which nothing escapes the drive to innovation, the rage for increased precision and power, in which stability, that sovereign good, is to be found only among decadent peoples—it is not enough to persevere in what is.

The English of thirty years ago did not realize, as they say, what the exercise of discipline, of calculation, of scrupulous and unlimited analysis, and an energy better applied than their own were preparing for them in every sphere.

The revelation came in a series of articles published in 1895 by The New Review *(which has since disappeared), directed by the good poet W. E. Henley. These articles were from the pen of Mr. Ernest E. G. Williams, and the title he gave to the series was a great success. Its three words "Made in Germany" were incorporated into law in a famous Act; at the same time they stuck in the English mind, and there they continued to have some influence until the eleventh of November, 1918.*

Surprise, excitement, and a kind of indignation arose when Mr. Williams brought out this collection of very detailed studies, dealing in turn with the various spheres of industry and commerce, and revealing the penetration and terrifying progress the rival had made in each domain.

Henley had the strange idea of asking a very young Frenchman, who was visiting London and had been recommended to him, to write for his New Review *a kind of "philosophical" conclusion to Mr. Williams' work of pure observation, with its assemblage of characteristic details. Nothing, until then, could have been further from the young Frenchman's mind than such a perplexing task, which certain very good reasons inclined him to accept, while reason alone commanded him to refuse. The reasons had the advantage of numbers. He improvised what he could, and here it is.*

During the last war, this essay was reprinted in the Mercure de France.

WE HAVE been stirred, we have been almost scandalized. A more disturbing Germany has been brought to light. The English are reading *Made in Germany* by Mr. Williams; the

French ought to be reading *Le Danger allemand* by M. Maurice Schwob.

She used to be a fortress and a school; now she is discovered to be an immense factory with enormous dockyards. We suspect too that there are connections between fortress, factory, and school; that these constitute different aspects of the same strong Germany. We are learning that the military victories which founded that nation are nothing compared to the economic victories she is now winning; already many of the world's markets are more hers than the territories she owes to her army.

So we perceive that both conquests are parts of the same system—the silent one superimposed on the resounding. We see that Germany has become industrial and commercial just as she became military—deliberately. We sense that she has spared no pains. If we wish to understand her new and far from imaginary greatness, we must conceive constant application, minute analysis of the sources of wealth, bold construction of the means of producing it, a rigorous survey of favored localities and serviceable roads and, above all, *total obedience*, the *constant devotion* to some simple, jealous, and formidable conception—strategic in form, economic in aim, scientific in its deep preparation and in the extent of its application. Such is the over-all view of German operations. If we turn now to concrete evidence, the documents, the diplomatic reports, the official statistics, we can admire at our leisure the perfection of detail, having glimpsed the majesty of the broad outline, and appreciate how—when everything knowable was known, when everything predictable had been predicted, when the formula for prosperity had been found— an activity, insinuating or brutal (in turn), both world-wide and continuous, radiated from every part of Germany to every part of the world, bringing about the *return* of maximum wealth from every part of the world to every part of Germany.

That activity is not, as ours is, a sum of individual activities that remain independent, sometimes contradictory, and blindly protected by the State, which dissipates its influence among all, unable to strengthen one without weakening the other. Hers is a massive power that acts like water, now by shock and fall, now by irresistible infiltration. A natural discipline links individual German activities to the action of the whole country, and so orders private interests that they join together and reinforce rather than reduce and contradict each other. This goes to the point of suppressing all rivalry between Germans when the foreigner—the enemy—is present.

And so it is a true union, an exchange of useful sacrifices, a combining of energies and skills for the common victory, producing, besides victory, a remarkable co-ordination among the fighting industries and among the various branches of the economic army of the *Vaterland*. Against that army we fight like savage tribes against organized troops.

Their action is not, like ours, haphazard. It is trained. All the sciences are made to serve it. It is guided by a careful psychology: rather than use force, it prefers to make itself desirable. Germany's customer is made to bless the German merchant and even German trade. More—the customer must be turned into a friend, a propagandist—which is a profoundly elegant operation. Now, this customer is well known. Thinking himself free, living in innocence, he has been analyzed without knowing it—though he has not even been touched. He has been classified and defined, along with everyone else in his town, his province, his country. What he eats, what he drinks, what he smokes, and how he pays, are known. And someone is thinking about his desires. At Hamburg or Nuremberg, someone has perhaps drawn graphs representing the exploitation of his slightest whims, his smallest needs. This man who imagines that he is living so personally, so intimately, would see himself, on those graphs, as a mere number among thousands of others who *prefer* the same liqueur or the same cloth as himself. For there, more is known about his own country than he himself knows. Someone else knows better than he the mechanics of his life, what he must have to live on, and what he needs to brighten his days a bit. Someone knows where his vanity lies, the luxuries he dreams of, and the fact that he finds them too expensive. What he wants will be manufactured for him, champagne out of apples, perfumes out of almost anything. The customer does not know how many chemists have him in mind. They will fabricate for him exactly what it takes to satisfy his purse, his desire, and his habits; he shall have something of perfectly average perfection. For it is through someone's servile obedience to his complex wish that he is to be caught.

To create this fabulous product—cheap, but a luxury, easy to procure, either traditional or fashionable—there is a whole army of scientists swarming in the numberless departments of industry. There is no article for which they cannot find a less expensive substitute, no new substance for which they cannot find a use, no science they cannot apply to industrial purposes. In a few years, Germany has become covered with factories, railways, canals. Her navy, too, starting from nothing, has already reached second place. She has admirable ships; she has dockyards and immense inland ports; her shipyards are always busy. She sends out astonishing travelers; their inquiries and exploits would do credit to diplomacy and science. She has information agencies in every country, she has merchants' associations that support those agencies, and associations of transport companies that carry the trade of those merchants.

The books I have mentioned contain the details of this gigantic *business*. They take us into the factories and the markets. They bring together amazing statistics. At one stroke they unroll the sequence of the years, and by this sudden elimination of time they show at a glance the fantastic expansion of German life. . . . The sensation we get is so powerful that we are led to conjecture about the future. The mind cannot stop at the last year entered in the statistics and on the balance sheet. It *automatically* foresees a still vaster development—imagining a continuation, a halt, a decline, a decadence. . . . The mind goes on, entirely free of the facts, following one of its own laws.

At this point, purely speculative research or intellectual inquiry begins. It is here that anyone who has absorbed the studies and investigations I have just referred to cannot fail to look further into the phenomena of German expansion for a more general meaning. It is the moment for *ideas*, for comparisons, for a tentative formulation of theories. All those enterprises, stratagems, public works, and schemes, all those patiently managed undertakings and their results, must, it seems to me, arouse in us—apart from national bitterness— that special admiration we cannot help but feel for any efficient mechanism, for any result that has been desired and rationally attained, step by step along the surest road. There is something intoxicating about being certain of an outcome, when it is obviously the result of premeditated action. In the present case the action is general, and regularly produces a general result unaffected by accidents and individual mistakes.

So, in Germany's success I see, above all, the success of a *method*. That is what arouses my admiration. Let us suppose that an ordinary man sets himself a difficult task—imposing but possible. We need endow him with no *genius*, no special insights, no inspired vision; merely with tireless, constant desire and average powers of reasoning, but with absolute confidence in reason. *That man will do what is required.* He will reflect without passion, he will carry out "enumerations so complete and reviews so general" that all objects and facts will serve him, and finally enter into his personal calculations. There is nothing that will not be seen either as favorable or unfavorable, to be either used or eliminated. Nothing will be overlooked. He will also observe the course of events, the *trend*. He will count and classify, then follow with action. Then victory. . . . But such a man would have too much to do. It takes a whole people. Every office is staffed by hundreds of persons. Every undertaking is supported by the whole mass—and that mass is naturally disciplined. Here the social vice of the intelligent, which is refusal of discipline, vanishes. A wonderful instrument remains: disciplined intelligence. And it is now nothing but an instrument.

I have taken the example of an ordinary man so as to show the almost impersonal power of methodical conduct, and the better to indicate the great good sense that consists in not speculating on the rare thing, the accident.

So there is at last one nation which, in the economic sphere, has tried unremitting reason, that is to say *method*, and the experiment has not come out too badly. It shows that the most important phenomena of life can serve as the basis and the subject of sustained mathematical operations—that life is not above human calculation. It can be dealt with. But only Germany could inaugurate such a system. With her it is not new, it is not surprising, it is organic. It has merely changed its object. First, Prussia was created methodically. Then she created contemporary Germany. At first, the system was political and military. Then, having fulfilled that destiny, it easily became economic, simply by applying itself. Modern Germany, the product of this system, is now continuing to develop it.

If, after reading *Le Danger allemand* or *Made in Germany*, we turn our heated and excited minds to the military history of Prussia from Frederick the Great to Field Marshal von Moltke, we cannot escape an impression of analogy, an idea of the system I have been speaking of. It will thus be seen how little exaggeration there is in the foregoing suggestions. Here as elsewhere, similar developments will be found: *perfect preparation*, a generally adequate execution—and always . . . results. I note that some of those results, bad in themselves, have turned out to be good, for they have all been subsequently used with great care—even defeat has provided experience, a *minimum gain*. This is a regular procedure, which is why I note it.

If now we look into the details of the Prussian military system we shall more and more easily recognize the main characteristics of the "Method." It must be sought in the preoccupation with strategy. Tactics are a matter of individuals, and embrace all the hazards of war. But the study of the future, carrying foresight as far as possible, carefully weighing the probabilities, everything that tends to reduce chance, to eliminate blind action—these are the remarkable qualities of the military method "Made in Germany." And war itself must no longer break out, end, or be carried on at the mere whim of events or passions. War will be made

53

rationally. It will be made for the purpose of putting down a competitor, of gaining access to ports. . . . It will be a great industrial operation, with its financial organization, its capital, its sinking fund, its insurance, and above all, its shareholders; for the indemnities and the millions in spoils will be spread over the whole of Germany, and will pay for new canals, new tunnels, new universities—all the means of recovery, so as to start again on a bigger scale.

On the field of battle, whether economic or military, a kind of general theorem dominates methodical action—that is, German action. The principle is certainly simple. It is the merest deduction in logic, almost nothing. Here it is: "The conqueror is always stronger than the conquered." This tautology must give food for thought to those who prefer to speak of combat with equal arms, for it can be expressed thus: "There is no such thing as equal arms." "Equal arms" is an old and quixotic idea. It is an incomprehensible superstition. . . . From the principle just stated, the practical rule for any battle can be deduced at once: *plan and bring about inequality*. Militarily, the aim is to have the better weapon, the faster march, the more favorable terrain, etc.; but the surest, the most obvious of all such means is superiority in numbers, that is to say, inequality mathematically visible, and really invincible if the margin is sufficient, if behind an army front there is an inexhaustible depth of reserves, of *Landwehr* and *Landsturm*. Commercially, inequality must be based on cheapness. The problem to be solved—which, in most cases, is solved—is that of making a cheaper product than the product under *attack*. The sciences, the various means of transport, and substitutes of every kind are to be employed. Where the art of war would concentrate the strength of armies and make the weight of huge battalions count, the art of commerce makes use of the lowest price, which has the same effect as superior numbers, crushing all resistance without fail and putting the enemy to flight.

The planning of military preponderance is the work of the general staff. In the conception of its famous headquarters is to be found the most striking example of method. They are really factories for turning out victory. Here we find the division of intellectual labor at its most rational, we find specialized minds fixing their constant attention on variations in the slightest possibilities of gain, we find *this kind of research extended to subjects that seem at first unsuited to technical study*, we find military science elevated to the plane of general policy—it becomes the general economy, for "war is made at all levels." The method is relentlessly applied against all countries. The territory of each is subjected to a complete analysis, science by science—from geology, which tells the nature of the terrain, its resources, its crops, its roadways and waterways, its natural defenses . . . to history, which furnishes the basis for psychological and political knowledge and reveals internal dissensions and indigenous ways of thought. All countries are thus classified and correctly defined. They are reduced to groups of abstractions that can enter into every kind of calculation; those great strips of land, really complex entities swarming with many different individuals, where customs seem so impenetrable to analysis, become *objects of thought*, manageable quantities, marked weights, all of which can be compared, to show which will be heavier or lighter in the scales of war. Each nation then is considered as a machine producing military energy and capable of being added or subtracted—in short, varied at the will of the expert.

The same kinds of generalization are applied by the commercial general staff. Let us now carry our exposition over into the practical field. The parallel continues.

The same method has created instruments of incomparable power and precision, without which the work of the army would be fruitless. One example is the information service. The military document and the economic document often seem to come from the same agencies. The unity of method suggests this. Besides, precisely because there is a method, the economic document is valuable to the military —and sometimes the military document is useful to certain industrialists. The transport service has the same dual importance. Rapid mobilization, necessary to insure the presence of effective numbers in the field, requires meticulous study to regulate the speed and distribution of transport. The requirements of safety, timing, and supply are discussed and planned in their smallest details. On them rests the whole of the future campaign.

German commerce, like the army, is served by the scientific organization of transport. If troops must arrive in great numbers, products must arrive as cheaply as possible. Hence a thousand private agreements, accommodations of every kind, mutual sacrifices to insure economic mobilization. The more we study the whole system of strategy built up by the military general staff, the more we see that the system of production and trade adopted by the German nation is another form of the same tendency, the more also we are led to imagine a single unified activity whose resources are varied, whose success is *regular*, whose aim is clear, simple, and vast. Calculated brute force advances because it neglects nothing, because it carefully divides all the difficulties so that its whole weight can be brought to bear on each of the smaller fragments. In peace it looks more frightening than in war.

Field Marshal von Moltke personifies the system. He was its director and example. It would seem that the profoundest of his schemes was: not to die indispensable. That is what distinguishes him from the great generals before him. It is the only thing he invented. He was above all a man, a man of trust, the engineer of German security and strength. The absurd desire to perform miracles—a desire that transfigures the whole of military history—ends with him. He deserves a special kind of admiration. The elements of his success are to be found in Frederick the Great, in Napoleon, and in the War of Secession (so filled with novelties). He took his method where he found it, and he always found it where victory was a regular result. In the depths of his mind dwelt a small number of almost crude moral or political ideas dominating all the rest, the sort of ideas that make the one who holds them so formidable to others, so headstrong, so incapable in himself of anything new, of any sublime variation.

But he had inquired into everything. He came to power nearly an old man; he had followed the course of the century's politics, had seen all Europe, appraised its armies, made the study of contemporary wars his avocation and understood them better even than those who conducted them. This man became a strategist. He dismissed the military ideas of his time. He took only its scientific ideas and its material progress, combining these with the best strategy of the past— that is to say, with what, to the end of time, it will be rational to do in war. In the use of the railways he saw the extension of Napoleon's famous rapid marches. He revised and perfected the ways of exploiting all the resources of an invaded country. He made war where he must; he terrorized the people so as to break down public morale. He multiplied the means of getting information, he listened to tips on public opinion and finance, to rumors, the newspapers, the demands of neutrals. . . . He was without passion, without genius, and surrounded with papers. The battlefield was not his battle-field: he should be pictured in a room, in a small occupied town, working with his faithful staff. He is diligently repairing the accidents and the disruptions caused by the sufferings of *others*. His is a face with no mouth; his whole figure is sealed tight, a fortress. Once, however, in 1870, he threw his phlegmatic wig in the air on receiving a telegram.

This one man's life is a complete lesson. It corresponds exactly to what we know of living Germany: the most *personal*—that is, systematic—aspect of his mind is to be seen even in her socialist organization. For that icy hero, the *true enemy was the accidental*. He warred against it, and his strength lay solely in method. Out of this comes a strange idea. Method calls for true mediocrity in the individual, or rather for greatness only in the most elementary talents, such as patience and the ability to give attention to everything, without preference or feeling. Finally, the will to work. Given these qualities, we have an individual who will always and inevitably get the better of any superior man whatever. The latter may think at first that his ideas have won out; then he will find them being circumscribed with ironical precision, then slowly modified and corrected to accord with a logic as faultless as it is unremitting. From the bold experiments of a Napoleon, a Lee, or a Sherman, the second-rate man draws the most solid precepts. He sees their actions in the light of an imperturbable scientific criticism. He refrains from relying on himself, which makes him more dependable than the great innovators. He methodically rejects sudden inspirations and unexpected discoveries. Time, which drains away the resources of luck and outlasts every flash of genius . . . time bears him out. In short, *he never dies*. After him, other second-rate men will come without fail to reiterate his career; it suits them best and elevates them most. When he is gone, everything remains: this is a source of great strength for the nation.

These considerations may serve to explain the distribution of men and the values they represent, in a modern State. Germany today shows superiority in practical achievements and in the sum total of her activity. But it would seem that the individual quality of her personnel is mediocre, stable, and moreover, perfectly suited to her general development. There, the heroic days are over, deliberately brought to a close. They are sometimes used for advertisement and appear in certain useful phrases, but that makes them even more remote. The great philosophers are dead, and there is no place any longer for great speculative scientists.* Both have given way to an anonymous and urgent science with no general critique or new theories, but fertile in patented products. And out of all the discoveries made by those superior men, nothing has been kept but what can be duplicated—nothing but what, when duplicated, adds to the resources of their mediocre successors.

That, however, is the new fact: a whole national body working as one. Rival energies are reconciled and directed outwards. The nation's undertakings follow one after another, and in each, everyone does his best. The classes of society and the various professions, in turn, take the lead. So, in the history of this century, Germany seems to have conformed to a carefully concerted plan. Each step has extended the scope of her national life. She has built herself up, ambition by ambition, and the symmetry of that progress gives to each of her enterprises the appearance of something arti-

* This sentence should be struck out; men like Einstein, Planck, etc., make it inaccurate, that is to say, unjust. [P.V., 1925]

ficial. For example, she formed her territory by means of well-aimed wars. Then she imposed an armed peace on Europe, which all the other States imagined was abnormal. Next she put her industry and her trade on a war footing. Then she simultaneously created her navy and her merchant fleet. Then she suddenly looked around for colonies. Like many another German enterprise, the famous affair of the Caroline Islands came like a thunderclap. It was one detail in some great project. Of the same nature was the Emperor's resounding telegram to President Kruger. England and the rest of the world were stirred. It was then realized that the Transvaal was already profoundly Germanized; Baron von Marschall's views on Delagoa Bay and Beira were called to mind; a whole scheme was revealed.* And recent books have likewise thrown a sudden light on the intensive development of the whole empire, the first fruits of premeditated war against the wealth of the whole world.

We must not disguise the fact that for the leading older nations the struggle will become more and more arduous. It has already assumed such a character that the very qualities those nations have always considered most propitious to their life and the principal source of their greatness have become signs of inferiority. For example, the habit of seeking to per-fect manufactured articles, of encouraging competition in home trade, of improving the workers' lot . . . these are all so many handicaps in the struggle. . . . But the question is a much wider one.

* In January 1896, people in the Cape were singing:
          "Strange German faces passing to and fro
          What have you come for, we should like to know?
          Looking mysterious as you join the train
          Say, now, you Uhlans, shall we meet again?"
                                        [P.V.]

Germany owes all to something that is most antipathetic to certain temperaments—particularly to the English and the French. That thing is *discipline*. It is not to be despised. It sometimes has another name: in intellectual matters it is called method, and I have already too often called it by that name. An Englishman or a Frenchman can invent a method. They have proved it. They can submit to a discipline; that, too, they have proved. But they will always prefer something else. For them, it is a last resort, a temporary measure or a sacrifice. For a German it is life itself. Moreover, Germany as a nation happens to be a recent entity. Now, all peoples who reach the estate of great nations—or who resume that status in an era when there are already great nations enough, more ancient and more civilized than they—tend to imitate in a short time what has required centuries of experience for older nations; and to this end they organize themselves entirely by deliberate method—just as every city deliberately constructed is always built to a geometrical plan. Germany, Italy, and Japan are examples of nations that have made a new beginning, very late, based on a scientific concept as accurate as it could be made by studying contemporary progress and the prosperity of their neighbors. Russia would offer the same example if her immense territory were not an obstacle to the rapid execution of such an over-all scheme.

In Germany, then, we find both a national character with a bent for organization and division of labor, and a new State wanting to rival and then to surpass the older States. It must be admitted, in fact, that she has displayed an uncommon energy and application in this task.

I have attempted to show the system behind this great undertaking by comparing its military aspect with its economic aspect, but examples from other domains would have brought us to the same conclusions. German science could have served as well. There too, segmentation, classification, the imposition of discipline on the objects of knowledge is the reigning principle. There too, amazing instruments multiply the output; laboratories, each more specialized than the last, the endless bibliographies, the lessons in *omni re scibili*, the men lost for a whole lifetime in the depths of obscure questions . . . all these constitute a national science completely at one with the country that generously supports it.

The question of method may therefore be considered in the abstract. Whenever the term is heard, everyone thinks of a kind of recipe or rule of thumb for passing from a definite given condition to another. Everyone thinks of method as excluding trial and error, and as consisting in the strict observation of certain prescribed rules adopted once for all, after initial and supposedly adequate reflection. And everyone is necessarily impressed by the power of such a thing. It is easy to show that with the help of procedures of this kind, the risks of an enterprise are reduced to a minimum. Surprises can be foreseen. A good method contains an answer to every possible case, and that answer is influenced as little as possible by sudden occurrences and unexpected problems. But of all these virtues, the following are the most interesting: a well-made method greatly reduces the need to invent. It makes research cumulative. For example: an industrialist wants to supply a particular country with a certain product. Instead of *inventing* the form of the object, he makes inquiries. The form is *given* by the taste of the future consumer. He then calls on the scientists in his pay to reduce, scientifically, the cost of production, etc. In the end, once the object has been manufactured, distributed, and sold, we shall see that it has required the successive application of nearly every kind of human knowledge, and that it has taken from each what was needed for the relative satisfaction of the customer and the absolute satisfaction of the manufacturer. Nothing is simpler than this operation, and yet only in Germany is it totally and rigorously applied. It is a matter, obviously, of conforming strictly to the nature of things, neglecting nothing: a matter of logic. The necessary must be done; and whereas the manufacturer who has no method will make a poor syllogism and do poor business when he asserts (let us suppose) that any *good* product must sell, therefore . . . etc., another, more astute, will reconcile logic and luck by refusing to leave the definition of a *good* product to vagueness and chance. He will go and find it in the book of the customer's heart.

In Germany, moreover, such accurate methods are easier to apply than in any other country. I spoke of discipline. There, it is native, and its virtue is to determine a man's place and the scope of his activity. In the army, as elsewhere, the idea is that each man must be able to do all he can. That is to be achieved only by constraint, and the limits imposed a priori on each are precisely based on the individual's highest yield. If a soldier must remain in the ranks, this is because, detached and on his own, he has less energy. A battalion of five hundred men is stronger than a gang of a thousand. The most striking fact about the German army, so planned and regulated in its smallest functions, is the intensive cultivation of limited initiative. Soldier and officer alike *must* do what seems right to them from moment to moment in combat. There is a kind of sliding scale that scientifically determines the freedom allowed to each successive rank. The results of discipline resemble those of method. Discipline multiplies individual efforts. It provides a simple, sure solution to every individual case. It absolutely compels the discovery of every-thing that can be discovered. All it asks is obedience and *never anything extraordinary*. It diminishes the role of chance.

The reader has perhaps accused me of exaggeration. To which I shall reply that if—even in Germany—things are not happening just as I have presented them, they will do so. I shall also say that I have merely faced what the whole world knows, and drawn my conclusions. The reader will perhaps have felt annoyed or uneasy at seeing me attribute over-whelming importance to method, so fatal to all imagination, so drab, on the whole. Yet I shall not conceal my opinion: I believe that what we are witnessing is only the beginning of method. I should like to show its possible, or if you will, its hypothetical role. We have seen it triumph in the political, military, economic, and scientific fields. . . . But the reader has taken refuge in the realm of the mind. He likes to think that metaphysics, the arts, literature, and the higher sciences remain inviolate, safeguarded by the exceptional quality of the men who excel in them or draw inspiration from them. The scientific method, for example, does not guarantee that the scientist will evolve a new theory or create a new image of the world. It may well increase his chances, but it can do no more than regulate what is *already* discovered. On the other hand, it is by unexplored paths and from uncontrolled events that ideas come. We have the theory of many a phe-nomenon, but we still lack the theory of theory. In literature and art, we have the same old apparent spontaneity, the same obscure origins, the same absence of any general procedures. The phenomena of choice, substitution, and association are scrupulously ignored. Yet I would wager that, in the minds of all those who are constantly engaged in doing or making something, some kind of method is created and developed. All the great inventors of ideas or forms seem to me to have employed individual methods. I mean that their power and their mastery were founded on the practice of certain *habits* and conceptions which disciplined their whole thought. Strangely enough, it is precisely the observable features of this inner method that we call their *personality*. It is of little importance, however, whether that method is or is not conscious. . . . All this would be a great subject for research, and for a book—*The Art of Thinking*—which has never really been written. The creators of formal logic were, of course, trying to do just that, but what they managed to discover was a wonderful instrument of analysis—not of discovery itself.

Suppose that book were written—and I see no reason why it should not be. Suppose, if you will, that several of those great minds I mentioned should, from practicing their inner methods, become conscious of them (such a thing has happened) and should, insofar as language will allow, divulge them. We should then see extended to the domain of intellect the same procedures that Germany now applies to the life of society. In literature we should see cases of methodical collaboration, with division of labor and the rest. Balzac tried it. In art we should see the artist working directly on each of the senses, on each of the psychological needs of his public, aiming straight at his man. Wagner did it.

Yet such a book would bring to a point of extreme precision the functioning of that curious law which makes a man a genius . . . to others. One is handsome, one is a genius only to others. Japan must think that Europe was made for her. And by virtue of a rational scheme already in operation in Germany, we should doubtless see the final triumph of all the mediocrity on earth. Method in all things would lead to a great saving in superior individuals. And what a curious result, if the results of that new order of things were in every way more perfect, more powerful, more pleasant than what we have today.

But . . . I do not know. I am merely unraveling consequences.

Unpredictability

[1944]

FOR AT least a hundred and fifty years, more than one people in the world has been a prey to the desire, or need—sometimes the rage—to refashion its social structure. More than one system born of reflective thought, the conscious fruit of someone's meditation, has offered to replace the various empirical solutions of the problem of getting men to live together. But it is only in the last few years that we have seen what had never been seen before: types of political, judicial, and economic organization conceived in complete spiritual sovereignty, by the light of a student's lamp—like poems or some other gratuitous labor of the intellect—energetically and literally applied, holding sway over immense territories and hundreds of millions of persons.

This is a tremendous "new fact."

I must explain what I mean by this. I was tempted to say "transcendent fact," but I dislike using certain terms whose overtones startle the mind—either hypnotizing it or putting it on guard, which are opposite but similar effects that should both be avoided.

I shall instance the history of science, which I divide into two periods, one ending in 1800, the other coming down to the present. Until the time of Volta, scientific research and speculation had from the beginning been practiced on identical phenomena. For example, no one had yet observed or even imagined that mechanical or chemical effects, or effects of light or heat, could occur along the length of an oddly twisted wire. In any case, the very idea then held of science implicitly excluded *the possibility of absolutely unpredictable facts*.

In that state of knowledge one could speak of the *universe* and the *unity of nature* without doubting that one knew what one was saying. There were such things as *time*, *space*, *matter*, *light*, and a quite precise distinction between the inorganic world and the other; and the expression *to know everything*, which is the complement of the word *universe*, seemed to have a meaning and to be a perfectly clear delimiting expression. Laplace was able to imagine a mind powerful enough to embrace, or to deduce from a finite number of observations, all possible phenomena past and to come.

But once an electric current was set going, the era of *entirely new facts began*. Each new fact was in its own way an attack on the theoretical structure of universal dynamics, which was thought to have been conceived in the widest possible generality. The very notion of *physical theory* has in the end been seriously, if not definitively, compromised. First of all, the mental imagery that had done such good service lost all its meaning once speculation was concerned no longer with subphenomena assumed to be similar to the phenomena directly observed, but rather with "things" that in no way resemble the things we know, since they only send us signals which we interpret as best we can. Furthermore, our language, and hence our logic, our concepts, our causality, our principles, have been found wanting: all this intellectual material will not fit into the nucleus of the atom, where everything is without precedent and without shape. Debatable probabilities have taken the place of definite and distinct facts, and the fundamental distinction between observation and its object is no longer conceivable.

What has happened? Simply that *our means of investigation and action have far outstripped our means of representation and understanding*.

This is the enormous *new fact* that results from all the other *new facts*. This one is positively *transcendent*.

The absolute novelties now coming into play in every order of things—for all things are now in some way dependent upon industry, which follows science as the shark its pilotfish —must inevitably result in a strange transformation of our notion of the future.*

The past (as history) is a piece of imagination based on records. The future used to be a personal combination of more or less documented imagining and whatever knowledge one might have of the present—a sort of impure computation in which one's feelings, hopes, and intuitions necessarily played an undetermined but considerable part. But all prediction is conservative; it demands that we be as we are in whatever future it constructs. That is why I wrote a long time ago: "We are backing into the future." The fact is that every idea that comes to us is compounded of ideas that have been used already. Every expression is an arrangement of already existing words. The possibility of imagining a future implies that this particular product of the mind may be resolved into molecules of memory. This is proclaimed in many a banal saying: "you can't change human nature," "history repeats itself," etc. And, *thanks to the crude simplifications that make the writing of history possible*, it used to be easy to perceive recur-

* Here, of course, is meant the *practical future*, where our plans, with their imaginary but presumably realizable details, are situated. [P.V.]

rence or repetition of events, analogous situations on which as many philosophies of history as you like could be founded, and nearly all the arguments and ready-made expressions that politics could need to get a notion of itself, to propose its programs and policies, justify its aims, and define its ideals. In those days it used to be commonly said that "history is experimental politics." This was a slight on the good name of true experiment; it confused the recital of facts of merely traditional importance with the direct observation of a *controlled* system in which well-defined acts can be performed to obtain a result or an answer of a definite kind. In any case, it would not seem that the race of men, whose history has been in the making for a very long time, have profited much from experience, or experiment, of the historical kind. The contrary might be maintained. I mention here, incidentally, that I do not know that anyone has made an "objective" study of political thought in general. It is a handsome subject. It would be interesting to show how the use of stimulants in the form of various abstract words, undefined but illustrated with bright or violent images, is indispensable. Also, it would be well to examine the controlling ideas, or rather metaphysical notions, for whatever they may be worth—for example, each of them presupposes a certain *conception of man*; the collation of these and the comparisons that would result could teach us something about the quality of the minds that make it their business to lead the world.

Thus, any prediction we are able to make can only be, by the very nature of all prediction, more or less historical; it excludes, consequently, everything that is so new that our vocabulary must lack even the words to conjecture about it. Our vocabulary is, in effect, only a form of history reduced to assimilable, usable, and living elements. Since, henceforth, we must deal with the *new*, of the irreducible type I have mentioned, our future is endowed with *essential unpredictability*, and this is the only prediction we can make.

All this smells of paradox. But if we return in thought to a slightly earlier time, which I lived through—say, 1890—and try to conceive what (1) the best minds of that time, and (2) the brains best equipped to produce the amazing developments in invention and organization that followed, could have imagined as likely to be seen in 1944, then we should find (1) that nothing in their circumstances gave them the slightest hint, the slightest idea of the prodigious novelties we now know, and furthermore (2) that nothing in the very substance of their creative sensibilities, their power to dream, presaged the totally unexpected things that in fact happened.

Unpredictability in every field is the result of the conquest of the whole of the present world by scientific power. This invasion by active knowledge tends to transform man's environment and man himself—to what extent, with what risks, what deviations from the basic conditions of existence and of the preservation of life we simply do not know. Life has become, in short, the object of an experiment of which we can say only one thing—that it tends to estrange us more and more from what we were, or what we think we are, and that it is leading us . . . we do not know and can by no means imagine where.

Remarks on Intelligence

[1925]

IT HAPPENS that someone has been asked whether there is a *crisis in intelligence*, whether the world is becoming stupid, whether there is a distaste for culture, whether the *liberal professions* are suffering, perhaps dying—their strength declining, their ranks thinning, their prestige gradually diminishing, their existence more and more thankless, precarious, and near its end. . . .

But this same someone is taken aback by such questions— he was far from thinking about them. He has to get hold of himself, turn around, and face them; he must rouse himself from other thoughts and rub the eyes of his mind, which are words.

"Crisis?" he says first of all, "what exactly is a crisis? Let's take a look at this term!" A crisis is the passage from one particular mode of functioning to another; a passage made perceptible by signs or symptoms. During a crisis, time seems to change its nature, duration no longer gives the same impression as in the normal state of things. Instead of measuring permanence it measures change. Every crisis involves the intervention of new "causes" that disturb the existing equilibrium, whether mobile or immobile.

How can we fit the idea of *crisis*, which we have now briefly reviewed, with the notion of *intelligence*?

We live on very vague, very crude notions, and, moreover, they live on us. What we know, we know from the operation of what we do not know.

Necessary and even sufficient though they are for quick exchanges of thought, there is not one of these incomplete and indispensable notions that can bear close inspection. Once our attention settles on one of them, we find in it a confusion of widely differing usages and examples that can never be reconciled. What was clear in passing, and readily *understood*, becomes obscure when we fix on it; what was whole breaks down into parts; what was with us is against us. A slight turn of some mysterious screw shifts the microscope of consciousness, adds the element of time to increase the magnifying power of our attention, and finally brings our inner confusion into focus for us.

Dwell, for example, however slightly, on words like *time*, *universe*, *race*, *form*, *nature*, *poetry*, etc., and you see how they divide to infinity, becoming incomprehensible. A few moments ago we were using them for understanding each other; now they change into means of confounding us. They took part, without our knowing it, in our plans and actions, like limbs so tractable that we forget them, until reflection sets them against us, transforms them into obstacles and difficulties. It seems, in fact, that words in movement and in combination are quite different things from the same words inert and isolated!

This general and indeed remarkable character of our instruments of thought is what engenders nearly all philosophical, moral, literary, and political life—all that activity which is as useless as can be, but also as helpful as can be in developing the subtlety, profundity, and proper action of the mind. Our enthusiasms and aversions depend directly on the vices of our language; its ambiguities promote differences, distinctions, and objections, all the sparring of intellectual adversaries. And fortunately they also prevent minds from ever coming to rest. . . . We can observe, as we turn the pages of history, that a dispute which is not irreconcilable is a dispute of no importance.

Intelligence is one of those notions that derive all their value from the other terms coupled with them, by affinity or contrast, in some discourse. It is contrasted at various times with sensibility, with memory, with instinct, with stupidity. Sometimes it is a faculty, at other times a degree of that faculty; occasionally it is taken to be the *whole* of the mind itself, and is given the whole vague lot of the mind's properties.

During the last few years this word, already encumbered with several quite different meanings, has, by a kind of contagion frequent in language, contracted a new and entirely foreign sense. I hardly think we are to be congratulated on extending the word *intelligence* to refer to a whole class of persons in society, and to translate in this way the Russian *intelligentsia*.

The phrase *crisis in intelligence*, then, may be understood to mean the deterioration of a certain faculty in all men; or only in those most gifted in that faculty, or who *should be*; or again, as a crisis in all the faculties of the average mind; or further, a crisis in the *value* and prestige of intelligence in our society, present or to come. And finally, it may also be seen, if we include the new meaning borrowed from the Russians, as a crisis affecting a class of persons with respect to the quality, the number, or the living conditions of its members.

It remains to be seen which of all these differently defined sorts of "intelligence" is the one supposed to be in jeopardy.

74

The someone being questioned sees at once five or six possibilities. He senses that the slightest further inquiry would bring out others. He wanders from one point of view to another, from crisis to crisis, from a crisis in one's *faculties*, to a crisis in *values*, to a *class* crisis.

I. *On Intelligence as a Faculty*

Let us first worry about whether man is becoming more stupid, more credulous, more weak-minded, whether there is a crisis in comprehension or imagination. . . . But who would warn him of it? Where are the signs of such a decline in mental power? And, if there were any such signs, who would have the legitimate right to interpret them?

Yet this strange question does not fail to suggest a few ideas. Here, for example, is a kind of problem that I shall state just as it comes to me. There can be no question of solving it.

It is to inquire in what way modern life—the inevitable machinery of modern life and the habits it inflicts on us—may modify on the one hand the physiology of our minds, our perceptions of all sorts, and above all what we do with our perceptions, or what becomes of them inside us; and, on the other hand, the place and function of the mind itself in the present condition of the human race.

We might examine, among other things, the development of all the means for gradually delivering the mind of its more painful labors: the recording devices to relieve the memory, the marvelous machines that spare the brain its labors of calculation, the symbols and methods making it possible to reduce a whole science to a few signs, the admirable facilities for making us *see* what formerly we had to *understand*, the direct registering of visual images so that they can be reproduced at will, whole sequences of them, according to the very laws of their proper succession—and how much else! We might ask whether so much help, so many powerful aids are not gradually reducing our powers of attention and the capacity of the average human being for mental effort, whether continuous or of specified duration.

Look at our arts, for example. We complain of having no style; we console ourselves by saying that our descendants will discover that we had one of some sort. . . .

But how could we possibly develop a *style*—that is, how would it be possible to acquire any consistent form, any general formula for construction and decoration (which are always simply the fruits of fairly long experience and of a certain continuity in taste, needs, and methods) when impatience, rapid execution, and sudden changes in technique beset all our works, and when *novelty* has for the past century been required of every production in every genre?

And, finally, where does this demand for the new come from? . . . We shall return to that, later on. For the moment let us leave such questions to multiply of themselves.

Impatience, I was saying. . . . Farewell to all labors endlessly slow: three hundred years for a cathedral, whose interminable growth curiously accommodated the successive variations and embellishments, actually seeming to seek and, as it were, unfold them high in the air! Farewell to painting as the final product of a long accumulation of transparent labors—of clear thin layers, each waiting week after week for the next, regardless of *genius*! Farewell to the perfecting of language, to meditating on literary problems, to the refinements that used to make a writer's works comparable at once to precious objects and to precision instruments! . . . We are now *committed to the moment*, to effects of shock and contrast, and almost compelled to seize upon whatever flashes into the mind from any chance stimulus, suggesting precisely that. We look for and appreciate the *sketch*, the *study*, the *rough draft*. The very notion of *completion* has almost vanished.

. . . .

Modern man is sometimes overwhelmed by the number and magnitude of his means. Our civilization tends to make it impossible for us to dispense with a whole system of miracles produced by the impassioned and combined labors of a great number of very great men and a host of lesser ones. Each one of us feels the benefit, bears the burden, and inherits the whole sum of this age-old capital of truths and formulas. Not one of us is able to do without this enormous inheritance; yet, not one of us is able to carry it. There is no man now living who can even conceive the crushing whole of it. That is why political, military, and economic problems are becoming so difficult to solve, why leaders are so rare, and errors of detail so far from negligible. We are witnessing the dying out of the *man who could be complete*, as well as of the man who could be materially self-sufficient. There is considerably less self-determination, there is a decline in the sense of mastery, and a corresponding increase of confidence in teamwork, etc.

The machine rules. Human life is rigorously controlled by it, dominated by the terribly precise will of mechanisms. These creatures of man are exacting. They are now reacting on their creators, making them like themselves. They want well-trained humans; they are gradually wiping out the differences between men, fitting them into their own orderly functioning, into the uniformity of their own regimes. They are thus shaping humanity for their own use, almost in their own image.

There is a sort of pact between the machine and ourselves,

like the terrible contract between the nervous system and the subtle demon of drugs. The more useful the machine seems to us, the more it becomes so; and the more it becomes so, the more *incomplete* we are, the more incapable of doing without it. There is such a thing as *the reciprocal* of the useful.

The most redoubtable machines, perhaps, are not those that revolve or run, to transport or transform matter or energy. There are other kinds, not built of copper or steel but of narrowly specialized individuals: I refer to organizations, those administrative machines constructed in imitation of the *impersonal aspects* of the mind.

Civilization is measured by the increasing size and number of such structures. They may be likened to huge human beings, barely conscious, hardly able to feel at all, but endowed to excess with all the elementary and regular functions of an inordinately oversized nervous system. Everything in them having to do with relations, transmission, agreement, and correspondence, is magnified to the monstrous scale of *one man per cell*. They are endowed with a limitless memory, as fragile as the fiber of paper. That is where they get all their reflexes, which are laws, regulations, statutes, precedents. Not a single mortal is left unswallowed into the structure of these machines, to become an object of their functioning, a nondescript element in their cycles. The life or death, the pleasures and works of men are details, means, incidents in the activity of these beings, whose rule is tempered only by the war they wage against each other.

Each of us is a cog in one of these groups, or rather we belong to several different groups at once, surrendering to each of them a part of our self-ownership, and taking from each a part of our social definition and our license to exist. We are all citizens, soldiers, taxpayers, men of a certain trade, supporters of a certain party, adherents of a certain religion, members of a certain organization, a certain club.

To be a member . . . is a remarkable expression. As a result of the more and more precise and minute analysis and carving up of the human mass, we have become somehow quite well-defined entities. As such, we are now no more than objects of speculation, veritable *things*. Here I must utter certain awkward words; I am obliged, though with a shudder, to say that *irresponsibility*, *interchangeability*, *interdependence*, and *uniformity*, in customs, manners, and even in dreams, are overtaking the human race. It seems that the sexes themselves are bound to become indistinguishable except in anatomical characteristics.

. . . .

All the foregoing remarks must now be brought together and related to our idea of *intelligence as a faculty*, and we must ask ourselves whether our regime of intense and frequent stimulants, disguised forms of punishment, oppressive utilities, systematic surprises, overorganized facilities and enjoyments is not bound to bring on a kind of permanent deformation of the mind, the loss of certain characteristics and the acquisition of certain others; and whether, in particular, those very talents which have made us desire all this *progress*, as a means of employing and developing themselves, will not be affected by abuse, degraded by their own handiwork, and exhausted by their own activity.

. . . .

Among living intellects, some spend themselves in serving

the machine, others in building it, others in inventing or planning a more powerful type; a final category of intellects spend themselves in trying to escape its domination. These rebellious minds feel with a shudder that the once complete and autonomous *whole* that was the soul of ancient man is now becoming some inferior kind of *daemon* that wishes only to collaborate, to join the crowd, to find security in being dependent and happiness in a closed system that will be all the more closed as man makes it more closely suited to man. But *this is to give a new definition of man*.

The whole disturbance in our minds today shows that great changes are coming in our idea of ourselves.

ii. *On Intelligence as a Class*

Let us consider for a moment what I shall call *intelligence as a class*.

Everyone is well aware that there is a certain tribe known for its special relation to the mind. No one can give a complete, simple, and definite description of it. It is a social nebula still to be resolved. But it is one of those vague nebulae that, the more closely they are looked at, the more their contours dissolve and their forms melt or slip away. There is always something left over that cannot be either fitted into their general shape or separated from it.

But this species complains; therefore it exists.

Intellectuals, artists, members of the various liberal professions . . . some of these are fairly useful to the animal life of society, others are useless (and among the latter perhaps are the most excellent, those who elevate our race a little, giving us the illusion of knowing, of advancing, of creating, of resisting our own nature). These days we hear that there is a depression in the value of such men, a decline in their prestige, that they are being exterminated by want. Their existence is, in fact, closely linked with a culture and a tradition which are threatened with an uncertain future, because of the present revolution in the affairs of the world.

Our civilization is taking on, or tending to take on, the structure and properties of a machine, as I indicated just now. This machine will not tolerate less than world-wide rule; it will not allow a single human being to survive outside its control, uninvolved in its functioning. Furthermore, it cannot put up with ill-defined lives within its sphere of operation. Its precision, which is its essence, cannot endure vagueness or social caprice; irregular situations are incompatible with good running order. *It cannot put up with anyone whose duties and circumstances are not precisely specified.* It tends to eliminate those individuals who from its own point of view do not exactly fit, and to reclassify the rest without regard to the past or even the future of the species.

It has already begun to attack the ill-organized populations of the earth. Moreover, there is a law (a corollary of that primitive law which turns need and the sense of power into aggressive impulses) decreeing that the highly organized must invariably take the offensive against the poorly organized.

The machine—that is, the Western World—could not help turning, one day, against those ill-defined and sometimes *incommensurable* men inside it.

So we are witnessing an attack on the indefinable mass by the will or the necessity for *definition*. Fiscal laws, economic laws, the regulation of labor, and, above all, the profound changes in general technology ... everything is used for counting, assimilating, leveling, bracketing, and arranging that group of indefinables, those *natural solitaries* who constitute a part of the intellectual population. The rest, more easily absorbed, will inevitably be redefined and reclassified.

A few remarks will perhaps clarify what I have just written.

It was never more than indirectly that society could afford the life of a poet, a thinker, an artist, whose works were unhurried and profound. It sometimes uses them as fake servants or nominal functionaries—professors, curators, librarians. But the professions are complaining; every government official's small freedom of decision is being more and more reduced; there is less and less *play* in the machine.

The machine neither will nor can recognize any but "professionals."

How is it to go about reducing everyone to professionals?

There is a world of fumbling involved in trying to determine the characteristics of those who specialize in the intellect!

Each of us uses whatever mind he has. An unskilled laborer uses his, *from his own point of view*, just as much as anyone else, a philosopher or a mathematician. If his speech seems crude and simple-minded to us, ours is strange and absurd to him, and everyone is an unskilled laborer to someone else.

How could it be otherwise? Besides, every man dreams at times, or gets drunk, or both; and in his sleep as in his cups, the ferment of images and their free and *useless* combinations make him a Shakespeare—to what degree is unknown and unknowable. And our laborer, stunned by fatigue or alcohol, becomes the playground of spirits.

But, you will say, *he does not know how to use them.*

Which simply means that he is a laborer from our point of view, though a Shakespeare from his own. When he wakes, all he lacks is knowing the name of Shakespeare and some notion of literature. He is unaware of himself as a creator.

And who would dare put, or not put, a fortune teller, a master of ceremonies, or a circus clown in the category of intellectuals?

Who will maintain that more intelligence is expended in one head than another; that more intelligence and more knowledge are needed in teaching than in business speculations or in creating an industry?

We must make up our minds to dabble in examples. While dabbling we sometimes splash up a few drops of light.

In questions that are by nature confused, and are so for everybody, I find it permissible—perhaps laudable—to present, just as they are, the tentative efforts, the half-formed notions, and even the rejected and refuted phases of one's thought.

I have sometimes seen very surprising definitions of the intellectual. Some include the accountant and exclude the poet. Some, if taken quite literally, are so inclusive that they are unable to exclude those beautiful machines so clever at making calculations or squaring curves, and far superior to many brains.

The thought of such computers suggests a reflection I shall make in passing.

There are certain intellectual activities that may lose *rank* because of progress in technical procedures. As procedures become more exact, as the practice of any profession is gradually reduced to the application of a specified number of means, precisely determined by examining the particular case, the personal value of the "professional" has less and less weight. We know the part played in a great many fields by individual skill and secret processes. But the progress I am speaking of tends to make results independent of these peculiar personal qualities.

If, for example, medicine were one day to reach, in diagnostics and the corresponding therapeutics, a degree of precision that reduced the practitioner's role to a series of definite and well-regulated acts, the doctor would become an impersonal agent of the science of healing, would lose the *spell* that comes from the uncertainties of his art and from that personal magic we inevitably suppose that he confers on it; he would henceforth take his place alongside the pharmacist, who has always ranked slightly below him because a pharmacist's operations are more *scientific*, being performed with scales.

It might be said—to use an odd term borrowed from the language of the law—that certain intellectuals are *fungible*, and others are not. The former are already caught up in the machine, or nearly so, being interchangeable and able to be taken one for another.

Of course, men are never absolutely interchangeable. When they are at all, it is only approximately.

Anyone who cannot be replaced by another—for the reason that he is unlike any *other*—is also one who fulfills no undeniable need. So we find in the intellectual population these two remarkable categories: *intellectuals who serve some purpose* and *intellectuals who serve none*. For man's bread, clothing, and shelter, and his physical ills, neither Dante, nor Poussin, nor Malebranche could do anything whatever. Conversely, bread, clothing, shelter, and the rest have a tendency to shun such men. The subsistence of the greatest men is scarcely to be justified by anything but *words*. . . .

The problem of *intelligence as a class* is far from being a new problem. The present situation, as they say, makes it extremely urgent, more urgent than ever before. Yet nothing is farther from being new.

Its history is easily summarized.

The opportunity or the necessity of rewarding the mind, in the guise of certain individuals, with a definite place in the social structure has in every age raised a fundamental difficulty which by its nature cannot be overcome. It lies not only in making the right definition but also in being obliged to make inevitable judgments of *quality*. At every attempt, we come up against the insoluble question of *gauging the best*. In scientific jargon we might call it *aristometry*.

Since everyone uses the mind he has, the first decision must show that there are certain uses of the mind that can serve to distinguish a particular class; but then, some account must be taken—or not taken—of the value of such uses, that is, of particular works and even of work in progress.

A bad mason is still a mason. A bad mechanic is still a mechanic. But an occasional artist, a scholar unacknowledged by other scholars, an unwitting philosopher, a self-styled poet . . . what are they?

And what is an artist, a scholar, a philosopher, or a poet during the period of his inner preparation or while he is waiting for recognition?

Descartes began publishing in his forty-eighth year; Johann Sebastian Bach, when he was over fifty. Until then, the former was an ex-soldier and *rentier*, the other a church organist. Two men who in the end produced works known to all, managed to subsist up to the moment of their flowering, thanks only to the *lack of precision in the social definitions of their day*.

I have a few more words to say on the history of this problem.

From time immemorial it has been given a simple, practical, even crude solution, which consists in defining intelligence by courses of study. The more a country holds on to its earlier ways—the more *static* it is—then the more heavily if not exclusively it relies on definition in terms of regular studies.

The *intelligence class* consists, in this case, of those who have completed their studies; and studies mean diplomas, i.e., material proof. Scholars, pundits, doctors, degree-holders of every sort . . . these make up the intellectual class; it can thus be described in the clearest possible way (*since it is a material way*), and its membership can very easily be counted. Such a system is excellent for preserving and transmitting knowledge, but mediocre if not bad for increasing it. It may also happen that the material proof turns out to be more durable than what it proves—than the zeal, curiosity, and mental vigor of the man who, by means of it, becomes a member of the lettered class.

Among the inconveniences of the system let us mention man's tendency to become fixed in an initial attitude. I am told that in America it is still possible to change careers at any age, to move from *liberal* to *manual* occupations, and vice versa.

From this ancient, practical distinction we pass easily to the modern notion of the *liberal professions*.

These, it seems, are the professions befitting a free man.

A free man was not supposed to live by the work of his hands. A liberal profession was the opposite of a manual profession. Yet a surgeon uses his hands, though gloved. A pianist lives by his hands; painters and sculptors try to live by theirs. All such professionals were formerly regarded as work-men. Veronese, when summoned to testify before the Inquisition at Venice, replied to the question about his profession: *Sono lavoratore!*

Today there is a profound change. The surgeon is no longer confused with the barber, nor the artist with the artisan; and the social hierarchy formerly based on esteem— on the supposed degree of nobility in occupations—has shifted. Surgery ranks much higher than a number of professions where the hands are used merely for writing.

You see how many unanswerable questions can be raised in the simple attempt to form a clear idea of the place accorded in the modern world to intellectuals, or to those who by tradition are presumed to be intellectuals. . . .

Every thrust at the difficulty brings an immediate riposte. Nevertheless, before gauging the extent and describing the symptoms of a particular illness, we must try to recognize its victims. As you have seen, I have tried in vain to characterize the intellectual, and to discover the sure marks of a liberal profession.

This kind of speculation is sometimes as diverting as a parlor game. It has the infinite range of the unexpected. The ultimate source of our surprise consists in the great fact I was dealing with a few pages back: a new society has caught an old society *flagrante delicto*; a more powerful and rigid organization is attacking a less powerful and looser organiza-tion. Analysis loses its way in the complexity of relations and distinctions it is obliged to note, or introduce, when it attempts to grapple with such conflicts. Although it feels deeply convinced of the frailty and even the futility of all moral and political speculation, it nevertheless perceives much that is very grave and almost painful in this *critical* disorder, which it cannot manage to define. Can we be sure that bread . . . that all the things essential to life may not one day be denied those men whose disappearance would in no way disturb the production of that bread and those things? The first to perish would be all those who cannot defend themselves by folding their arms. The rest would do likewise, or go back to practical work, overtaken by the rising poverty; and the progress of their extermination would, for some supreme observer, demonstrate the actual hierarchy of the true needs of human life at its simplest.

Politics of the Mind

[1932]

I PROPOSE to evoke for you the disorder in which we live. I shall try to show you the reactions of a mind as it observes that disorder: how, when it has taken the measure of what it can and cannot do, it turns inward to reflect, and tries to picture for itself that chaos, to which, by its very nature, it is opposed.

But the image of chaos is chaos. Disorder is therefore my first point; it is this I ask you to think about. A certain effort is needed, for we have come to be accustomed to it, we live on it, we breathe it, we add to it, and sometimes we feel a real need for it. We find it all around us and within us, in the newspapers, in our daily life, in our manners, in our pleasures, even in our knowledge. It sustains us; and what we have ourselves created is now dragging us whither we do not know and do not wish to go.

Our present situation, which is our own handiwork, necessarily prepares the way for a certain future, but a future we cannot possibly imagine, and that is a great novelty, deriving from the very novelty of the present we live in. We cannot, or can no longer, deduce from the past even a glimmer, a faintly probable image of the future, since in a few decades and at the expense of the past (that is, by destroying it, refuting it, deeply modifying it) we have recast, reconstructed, and implemented a state of things whose most remarkable characteristics are without precedent or example.

Never was there a transformation so prompt and so profound: the earth has been entirely reconnoitered, explored, exploited, I would even say entirely appropriated; the most distant events are now known on the instant; our ideas about matter, time, and space, and our power over them, are all conceived and used quite otherwise than before. Where, now, is the thinker, the philosopher, the historian (even the profoundest, wisest, most erudite) who would today risk making the slightest prophecy? Where is the politician or the economist we would trust, after the errors they have made? We can no longer clearly distinguish between war and peace, abundance and want, victory and defeat. . . . And our economy fluctuates every day between an unlimited increase in *tokens* of exchange and a sudden return to the primitive system of savages: barter.

Sometimes, when I think of the condition of men and things, at once so brilliant and so dark, so active and so abject, I remember an impression I once had at sea. It happened that a few years ago I was on a voyage with a naval squadron. The squadron, having started from Toulon and heading for Brest, was suddenly, on a fine day, caught in a fog in the dangerous, rock-strewn approaches to the Île de Sein. Six battleships and about thirty smaller ships and submarines were suddenly blinded and brought to a halt, at the mercy of wind and current in the midst of a field of reefs. The least shock could have *upset* those citadels of armor and artillery. The impression was striking: those great ships, prodigiously equipped, manned by men of courage, knowledge, and discipline, with everything that modern technology can offer in the way of power and precision at their disposal, suddenly reduced to impotence in the half-light, condemned to anxious waiting by a bit of mist that had formed over the sea.

This contradiction is much like the one we are faced with in our time: we are blind and impotent, yet armed with knowledge and power, in a world we have organized and equipped, and whose inextricable complexity we now dread. The mind strives to clear up the disturbance, to foresee what it will bring forth, to discern in the chaos the imperceptible currents, the lines that will eventually cross to become the happenings of tomorrow.

At times it wants to keep whatever of the past seems essential, what it knows, and thinks civilized life cannot do without. At times it resolves to make a clean sweep, to construct a new system out of the world of man.

On the other hand, the mind must think of itself, of the conditions of its own existence (which are also the conditions of its growth), of the dangers that threaten its virtues, powers, and possessions: its freedom, its development, its depth. These are the two preoccupations which, as I was inquiring into them, suggested my somewhat vague and mysterious title, *politics of the mind.*

I should like simply to show that these questions exist. I have no intention of going into them deeply; no intention even of trying to circumscribe a subject of such vast extent, which, far from becoming simpler and clearer upon meditation, only becomes the more complex and cloudy as our attention dwells on it. If we explore even superficially all our spheres of activity, the fields of human ability and knowledge, we observe in each the signs of crisis: an economic crisis, a crisis in science, a crisis in arts and letters, a crisis in political freedom, a crisis in manners. . . . I shall not go into details. I shall simply point out one of the remarkable features of this situation: *the modern world with all its power, its prodigious technological capital, its thorough discipline in scientific and practical methods, has never managed to provide itself with a system of politics, a code of morals, an ideal, or a code of civil or penal laws in harmony with the ways of life it has created, or even with the ways of thought gradually being imposed on all men by the wide dissemination and development of a kind of scientific spirit.*

Everyone today who is more or less informed of the works in critical analysis that have renewed the foundations of science, elucidated the properties of language, the origins of the forms and institutions of social life, understands that every notion, principle, or *truth* as one used to say, is subject to review, revision, recasting; that every action is conventional, that every law, written or otherwise, is no more than approximate.

Everyone tacitly agrees that the *man* in question in constitutional or civil law, the pawn in political speculations and maneuvers—the *citizen*, the *voter*, the *candidate*, the *taxpayer*, the *common man*—is perhaps not quite the same as the man defined by contemporary biology, psychology, or even psychiatry. A strange contrast is the result, a curious split in our judgment. We look on the same individual as both responsible and irresponsible; we sometimes consider him irresponsible and treat him as responsible, depending on which of these fictions we adopt at the moment, whether we are in a juridical or an objective frame of mind. In the same way, we find that in many minds faith coexists with atheism, anarchy of feeling with doctrinal views. Most of us have several different opinions on the same subject, and these may easily alternate in our judgments within a single hour, depending on the stimulus of the moment.

These are sure signs of a *critical phase*—that is, of a kind of inner disorder defined by coexisting contradictions in our ideas and inconsistencies in our actions. Our minds, then, are full of tendencies and thoughts that are unaware of each other; and if a civilization's *age* is to be measured by the number of contradictions it contains, by the number of incompatible customs and beliefs to be found in it, all modifying each other, or by the multiplicity of philosophies and systems of aesthetics that coexist and cohabit in the same heads, it must be agreed that our civilization is one of the most ancient. Do we not constantly find several religions, several races, several political parties represented in one family . . . and in one individual a whole armory of latent discord?

A *modern man*, and this is what makes him modern, lives on familiar terms with many contraries waiting in the penumbra of his mind and coming by turns onto the stage. That is not all. We seldom notice these inner contradictions, or the coexisting antagonisms around us, and only rarely does it occur to us that they have not always been there. Yet it would suffice to remember that tolerance, which is freedom of opinion and belief, is always a tardy thing; it can be conceived and introduced into law and manners only in an advanced era, when minds have progressively enriched and enervated each other by exchanging their differences. Intolerance, on the contrary, is a terrible virtue of *purer* times. . . .

I have dwelt on this characteristic, for I see in it the very essence of modernity. I see in it also one of the causes of the great difficulty, or rather impossibility, of representing the present world on a single plan and a single scale. We can hardly think about it without getting lost. So it is useless to try, on the basis of a knowledge of history, to conjecture what will be the sequel to our state of general bewilderment. I have already said that the extraordinary number of novelties introduced into man's world in so few years has very nearly abolished all possibility of comparing what happened a hundred and fifty years ago with what is happening today. We have introduced new forces, invented new means, and formed entirely different and unexpected habits. We have canceled values, dissociated ideas, destroyed sentiments that seemed unshakable, having survived twenty centuries of vicissitudes; and to talk about such a novel situation we have only age-old notions.

In short, we are faced with confusion in the social system, in the verbal material and the myths of all kinds inherited from our ancestors, and in the conditions in which we live—conditions that are intellectual in origin, quite artificial, and moreover essentially unstable, for they are directly dependent on further and ever more numerous creations of the intellect. Here we are then, a prey to this confused mixture of *boundless hopes* (*justified by our incredible achievements*) and *immense disappointments* or *sinister expectations* (*equally justified by our incredible failures and catastrophes*).

· ·

But I must now complete this panorama of disorder, this composition of chaos, by picturing for you something that both observes and contributes to it, can neither endure nor deny it, and that, by its nature, never ceases to be divided against itself. I mean the *mind*.

By this word "mind" I do not at all mean a metaphysical entity; I mean quite simply a *power of transformation* which can be isolated and distinguished from all other powers simply by considering certain events around us, certain transformations in our surroundings that can be attributed only to a very different kind of action from that of the known energies of

Nature; for it consists, indeed, either in setting such given energies against each other, or in combining them.

The opposition or coercion involved is such that it results either in saving time or saving our strength or increasing the power, precision, freedom, or length of our lives. So you see, there is a way of defining the mind that does not involve any metaphysics, but simply gives that word the irreproachable status of a notation, making of it somehow the symbol of a group of quite objective observations.

Certain of the transformations worked by this power define a higher sphere. The mind not only applies itself to satisfying instincts and indispensable needs, it also makes a practice of speculating on our sensibility. Is there any more remarkable feat of transformation than that which takes place in the poet or the musician when they transpose their affections and even their sadness and distress into works, poems, musical compositions—the means of preserving and communicating the whole of their sensory life by the roundabout way of technical artifice? And, just as the mind can change its sorrows into works of art, so it has managed to change man's leisure into games. It changes simple wonder into curiosity or a passion for knowledge. The amusement it finds in making combinations has led it to build profoundly abstract sciences. The first geometricians were doubtless men whose calculations and figures diverted them in private, and who had no idea that one day the results of their austere pastimes would have a use: that of elucidating the structure of the world and discovering the laws of Nature.

In the same way, it was by a unique exploitation of the resources of the transforming mind that fear itself came to give birth to astonishing creations. Fear built temples—fear itself was changed at last into those wonderful supplications in stone, those magnificently meaningful structures that are perhaps the highest human expression of beauty and will. So, out of the affections of the soul, out of leisure and dreams, the mind makes higher values; it is a veritable philosopher's stone, the transmuting agent of all material or mental things.

The single characteristic I have selected to define it, and the examples I have just given, now make it possible for me to say that man's mind has involved him in an *adventure*, of a kind that seems bent on leaving further and further behind the original conditions of man's life, a kind that seems endowed with a paradoxical instinct tending in quite the opposite direction from all the other instincts—since the latter, on the contrary, always tend to bring the human being back to the same point and the same condition.

It is this strange instinct that tries somehow to remake the milieu in which we live, and to give us occupations that are sometimes excessively remote from those imposed on us by the pure and simple concern for our animal existence; it creates new needs, it gives us numerous artificial needs, it introduces alongside the natural instincts I mentioned, alongside the several goads of vital necessity (instinct means *goad*), many other impulses. In particular it has created a quite remarkable need to accumulate experience, to assemble and record the various kinds, to make structures of thought from them, and even to project them beyond the present, as though trying to get hold of life where it does not yet, or can no longer, exist.

Allow me to point out in passing one of humanity's most extraordinary inventions (and it is not a recent one). I am thinking quite simply of the invention of the *past* and the *future.* These are not natural notions; natural man lives in the moment, like an animal. The nearer a man is to Nature, the less do past and future figure in his mind. An animal doubtless feels that it exists between a minimum of past and a minimum of future—just that bit of each needed to sustain a desire until a sensation satisfies it, or to sustain a sensation of need until an act fulfills it. Duration is here reduced to the intervals of tension or action originating in a stimulus and ending in a quick organic response. Of course various incidents may come in between these limits of duration; but it is always *by the quickest way* that the irritated sensibility excites an act to appease it.

It is different with man: by expanding the moment, by using imagination to generalize the present, by a sort of abuse, man *creates time*; and in doing so he not only sets up perspectives before and after his intervals of reaction but, what is more, *he lives but very little* in the moment itself. His principal home is in the past or in the future. He never confines himself to the present except when forced to do so by a sensation: pleasure or pain. It may be said of man that *he continually feels the need of what does not exist*. This is a non-animal condition, and wholly artificial since in fact it is not absolutely necessary to life. No doubt the invention of "time" can often be useful. But to use it is, in itself, somehow contrary to Nature. Nature is indifferent to individuals. If man prolongs or betters his life he is acting *against Nature*, and his act is of a kind that sets mind in opposition to *life*.

Now, the intellectual exercise of foreseeing is one of the essential bases of civilization. Foresight is at once the origin and the instrument of all undertakings, large or small. It is also, presumably, the foundation of all politics. It is, in short, a psychic element that has become indispensable to the organization of human life. To an observer watching from outside humanity, man would generally seem to act without any visible aim, as though seeing into another world, as though responding to the influence of invisible things or hidden beings. *Tomorrow* is a hidden potentiality. Those are some examples. . . . Foresight is the inner being, as it were, of every action which that observer I mentioned cannot understand, because he can see only what is visible.

Furthermore: not only has man acquired the ability to take leave of the present moment, thus dividing against himself, but he has at the same time acquired another remarkable ability, though one not equally developed in all individuals. I mean that, in varying degrees, he has become *conscious of himself*. This consciousness makes it possible for him to be detached at moments from *everything*, even from his own personality; the *self* can sometimes look on its own person almost as some strange object. Man can observe himself (or thinks he can); he can criticize himself, and control himself. This is an original creation, an attempt to create what I shall make bold to call *the mind within the mind*.

Let us add to this summary description of the mind as I have conceived it, and as I have just now presented it—in terms of such firsthand observations as the creation of *time*, the creation of a *pure self*, a self distinct even from identity, even from memory, even from the personality of the subject—let us add to these the notion of the richest resource man has discovered in himself: that *universality* which he feels is his, and on which all his speculative life, all his philosophic or scientific or aesthetic life depends. Even in the practical sphere, the projection of his activity and his cravings, the opportunities he must grasp, the game he must play, the road he must follow, the

98

precautions he must take . . . all this requires developed skill, practice, a whole training in the *possible*. The possible is a kind of faculty.

Man speculates: he makes plans and theories. What is a theory if not precisely the *use of the possible*? Is not the practice of foresight, which I spoke of just now, a remarkable application of this faculty? But there is a particular kind of foresight that I must mention in passing: not only does the mind try to foresee external phenomena and events, but it strives to foresee itself, to anticipate its own operations. It strives to predict all the consequences of the data gathered by its own act of attention, and to discover the law they obey. This is because there is in the mind some peculiar horror (I nearly said *phobia*) of repetition. *What is repeated in the mind never belongs to the mind itself.* The mind tends never to repeat; it detests reiteration, although it sometimes reiterates by accident. On the contrary, it always tends to find a law of sequence, to approach the limit (as mathematicians say)— that is, to dominate, surmount, and somehow forestall a prospective repetition. It tends to reduce infinity to a *formula* by identifying the elements that make it up. The science of mathematics is at bottom, and to a large extent, only a science of pure repetition. It grasps the mechanism of repetition and summarizes it.

So the mind seems to abhor and shun the very process of deep organic life—which (unlike the mind) *requires* repetition, requires that the elemental acts on which vital exchanges depend be repeated: *our life is based on the regular recurrence of a few reflexes.* . . . Knowledge, on the other hand, implies a will opposed to the particularity, the singularity of moments. Knowledge tends to absorb the particular case into the general law, repetition into formula, differences into averages and large numbers. In doing so, the mind stands quite in opposition to the behavior of our living machine.

Notice that *living*—in spite of widely held opinion, in spite of the notion of life we get from newspapers, theaters, and novels—is an essentially monotonous practice. A show or a book is mistakenly said to be "living" when it is rather disorderly, when it gives us the unexpected, the spontaneous, in flashes and exciting effects. . . . These are only superficial characteristics, the fluctuations on the surface of sensibility; but the basis beneath these semblances, the substance of such accidents, is a system of periods or cycles of transformation that take place outside our consciousness and generally in the dark depths of our sensibility.

In the mind itself, our memory, our habits, our automatisms of every kind, are the signs of that deep, quiescent life; but the infinite variety of external circumstances finds in the mind resources of a superior order. In particular, the mind creates both order and disorder, for its business is to provoke change. In doing so, it develops within an ever vaster domain the fundamental law (or at least what I consider to be the fundamental law) of sensibility, which is to introduce into the living system an element of imminence, of always impending change.

Our sensibility has the effect of interrupting, at every moment, a kind of sleep that tends to overcome us, in harmony with the deep monotony of the functions of life. We have to be shaken, warned, waked up at each instant by some irregularity, some event in our surroundings, or some change in our physiological rhythm; and we have organs, a whole specialized system that calls us back unexpectedly and frequently to *the new*, prompting us to find the adjustment that suits the circumstances, to find the attitude, the act, the movement, the twist that will annul or accentuate the effects of novelty. This system is our senses.

The mind, then, borrows from sensibility (which provides the initial spark) that trait of changeableness required to set in motion its power of transformation.

An animal, quietly at rest, hears an unusual noise; this is an *event*. He pricks up his ears, straightens his neck; anxiety takes hold of him; the *power of transformation* spreads all over his body, brings him to his feet; his ear finds the direction, and he is off. *It took but a murmur*. In the same way, a mind that is alert to phenomena, a mind in which familiarity has not dulled sensitivity, is aroused, *caught* by some simple event (an object falling); intellectual concern overtakes it, is communicated to its whole potential of questions and conditions. . . . Newton lived for twenty years in the forest of his calculations.

A further remark: the work which the mind spurs us to do, the modifications it imposes on its surroundings (whether Nature or human beings), these are the means by which the mind tends to communicate to human beings, and to Nature, precisely the same characteristics it recognizes in itself. Have you noticed that all our inventions tend either to save our energies, or to save repetition (as I have said), or, again, to remove our bodies from their natural conditions, to impose on them, for example, speeds of a magnitude constantly approaching the mind's speed of perception and conception?

People used to say "as quick as thought." Rapidity seemed to belong to perception. But today we know many kinds of speed greater than that. In the time that elapses between the sight of an object and the memory or recognition it evokes, light has traveled thousands of miles and our car has done ten yards on the road. Thought, then, seems to have cleverly found the means of making things go as fast as itself. This is one way in which the functional properties of the mind have influenced the course of invention.

But my aim is not only to characterize the mind; it is above all to show what it has made of the world and how, in particular, it has produced modern society, in which both order and disorder, equally and for the same reason, are its handiwork. In the human world, the mind finds itself surrounded by other minds; each is, as it were, the center of a multitude of others like it, it is *unique* and yet it is only a unit in that indeterminate number; *it is at once incomparable and commonplace*. Its relations with all the others are one of its most important occupations. These relations are part of the contradiction I just pointed out. On the one hand, the mind is opposed to the mass: it wants to be itself, and even to extend, endlessly, the domain in which the *self is master*. On the other hand, it is forced to recognize society, a world of wills and human hopes all limiting one another; and sometimes it wants to perfect, at other times to destroy, the order it finds there.

The mind abhors groups; it does not like political parties; it feels itself diminished by the agreement of minds; indeed, it feels that it gains something from disagreement with them. A man who needs to think like his fellows is perhaps less *intelligent* than the man who detests conformity. Besides, we know very well that all agreement is unstable. We know that division lurks in all groups: schism, objection, distinction are, for the mind, acts of vitality that never fail to crop up, once agreement has been reached. The mind, then, regains its freedom by way of mental reservations and afterthoughts; it stands up even against the facts, against the evidence; it is, above all, the rebel, even in the act of bringing order. That is because it conceives *the real* as a kind of disorder to be brought to an end. But, in the world today, the mind requires no great effort to find a use for its constructive instinct. The political scene offers endless opportunity.

All politics imply a certain idea of man. In vain do we limit political objectives, make them as simple or as crude as possible, all politics still imply a certain idea of man and of the mind, and a conception of the world. Now, as I have already indicated, in the modern world the difference between the idea of man proposed by science and philosophy and the idea of man implied in our legislation and all our political, moral, or social notions, is increasing. There is already an abyss between them. . . .

If we should translate anything of a social and moral order into the precise terms used in science, the discord between the two ideas would be obvious: one would be the product of recent objective research, founded on *verifiable* evidence (which is the exact meaning of the world "scientific"); the other, a vague and confused notion, in which ancient beliefs, the customs of every age, abstractions from a thousand years back, the economic and political experience of many peoples, and a host of more or less venerable sentiments, all oddly intermingle and combine. Let us give an example: if we tried to apply, in the realm of politics, the ideas about man which we find in the current doctrines of science, life would probably become unbearable for most of us. There would be a general revolt of feeling in the face of such strict application of perfectly rational data. For it would end, in fact, by classifying each individual, invading his personal life, sometimes killing or mutilating certain degenerate or inferior types. . . .*

* A recent piece of legislation in a certain foreign country has fulfilled this prediction by prescribing several such strictly rational measures. [P.V.]

I do not know whether man will ever consent to so purely rational an organization; I chose this example, purposely exaggerated, only to show the remarkable contrast between certain conceptions now coexisting and competing in our minds, each with its own strength, and linked either with tradition or progress. Actually, this antinomy between scientific *truth* and political *reality* is something quite new. The gap did not always exist. There have been periods when the conception of man held by the judge and the statesman, or embodied in laws and customs, and that formulated by the philosophy of the time were not contradictory.

. . . .

I said just now that the mind is characterized by a power of transformation that tends to alter the original animal condition of the species, and that as a result it has managed to build for itself a kind of world quite different from the world as it originally was. It is not surprising therefore that the mind is a prey to numerous perplexities brought on by the conflicts and contradictions that inevitably arise between the kind of progress I just spoke of and the fundamental nature of man, the nature he started with. Side by side with the real enigmas that face us in things themselves, we find others posed by our own handiwork, by the accumulation of our own creations.

A great many of our present difficulties derive from the vigorous survival of a kind of mystique or mythology which is less and less in agreement with facts, but which we do not know how to get rid of. We constantly feel both its dead hand and the necessity for it. A struggle is going on in us between the past, represented by that mythology, and a sort of future trying to take shape in us. Never has the struggle between yesterday and tomorrow raged so furiously as today. You might indeed discover a few faint suggestions of it, certain *prefigurations*, in history; for example, at the end of ancient times, at the beginning of Christianity, at the time of the Renaissance, or at the moment of the French Revolution.

But the scale of events has curiously altered. The further we go, the more we feel the widening gap between the two aspects of the mind's activity, the one of transformation and the other of preservation.

Let me first say that the whole social structure is founded on *belief* and *trust*. All power is based on these psychological traits. It may be said that the *social*, the *judicial*, and the *political worlds*, are essentially *mythical worlds*, that is, worlds in which the constitutive laws, principles, and relationships are not the result of observation or notation or direct perception, but, on the contrary, draw their vitality, their strength, their power to compel or restrain, from us; *and their vitality and power are all the greater as we are the more unaware that they have their origin in us, in our own minds.*

To believe in the human word, spoken or written, is just as indispensable to human beings as to trust in the firmness of the ground. Certainly we do doubt it here and there, but we can doubt it only in particular cases.

An oath, a contract, a signature, the institution of credit, and the relations which all these imply, the substance of the past, our sense of the future, the teachings we receive, the plans we make—all these things are by nature wholly mythical, in the sense that they are wholly based on the cardinal principle of our minds, *not to treat as things of the mind things that are of the mind only.*

Now, the essential character of our indispensable mythology is this: it is the means of making *unequal* exchanges—of exchanging spoken or written words for merchandise, of exchanging a bird in the hand for a bird in the bush, of exchanging present and certain for future and uncertain, and what is still more remarkable, of exchanging trust for obedience, enthusiasm for renunciation and sacrifice, sentiment for action.

In short, of exchanging the present, the palpable, the ponderable, the real . . . for imaginary advantages. But the growth of the positivist mentality, a growth resulting, as you know, from the ever tighter organization of the world, where measurable things more and more dominate the scene, where the vagueness of *vague things* is more and more obvious . . . the growth, as I said, of the positivist mentality is undermining the ancient foundations of society.

It must be acknowledged that our ruin has been hastened by the greatest minds (Voltaire, for example). Even in the sciences the task of criticism has proved singularly necessary and fruitful. The greatest minds are always skeptical minds. Yet they do believe in something: *they believe in whatever makes them greater*. This was the case, for example, with Napoleon, who believed in his star, that is, in himself. Now, not to believe in the common beliefs is obviously to believe in oneself, and often in oneself alone.

But to clarify this glimpse into the *fiduciary life* of the world, founded on confidence in man and in the future, and to give you a sense of the very real importance of the imaginary, I should like to show you how *power* itself, which is ordinarily thought to result from force, is essentially a spiritual value.

Power has only the force we are willing to attribute to it; even the most brutal power is founded on belief. *We credit it with the ability to act at all times and everywhere, whereas, in reality, it can only act at one point and at a certain moment.* In short, all power is exactly in the position of a bank whose existence depends on the sole probability (incidentally, very great) that all its clients will not come at once to draw out their deposits. *If, either constantly or at any particular moment, a certain power were summoned to bring to bear its real force at every point in its empire, its strength at each point would be about equal to zero.* . . .

Notice too (and this is an even more interesting consideration), that *if all men were equally enlightened, equally critical, and above all equally courageous, no society would be possible!* . . .

Trust, credulity, inequality of intellect, and fear in a thousand forms are here equally indispensable. And to these essentials must be added greed and vanity—and other virtues —the condiments, the psychological accessories to those psychological bases of society and politics.

But I want to give you a rather striking (though purely fanciful) illustration of the fiduciary structure which is necessary to the whole edifice of civilization, and which is the work of the mind.

Suppose (and this supposition is not mine; it was made, I think, by an English or an American writer whose name I have forgotten, and whose book I have not read; I am merely borrowing the idea, which I found a long time ago in some review of the book) . . . well, the author in question supposes that a kind of mysterious disease attacks and quickly destroys all the paper in the world. No defense, no remedy; it is impossible to find any means of exterminating the microbe or of countering the physiochemical phenomenon attacking the cellulose. The unknown destroyer penetrates drawers and chests, reduces to dust the contents of our pocketbooks and our libraries; every written thing vanishes.

Paper, you know, plays the part of a storage battery and

a conductor; it conducts not only from one man to another but from one time to another, carrying a *highly variable charge of authenticity or credibility*.

Imagine, then, that paper is no more: no more bank notes, bonds, treaties, records, laws, poems, newspapers, etc. At once the whole life of society is struck down, and out of the ruins of the past we see the future emerging, the potential and the probable—*pure reality*.

Everyone immediately realizes that he is reduced to his own sphere of perception and action. In each individual, future and past draw incredibly close together; we are reduced to the radius of our senses and our immediate acts.

It is easy to imagine this example of the enormous role played by verbal and fiduciary values. Nothing could more impress upon us the fragility of world order and the *spiritual nature* of social order than this fantastic supposition.

But I shall now make another, a far less fantastic supposition, which ought on that account to be more impressive: instead of decaying from some disease, a sort of tuberculosis of paper (that fragile basis of so many things), suppose now that the *basis of that basis* should weaken and collapse—I mean the trust, the confidence, the credit we give to written paper, thus giving it all its value. Such a thing has happened before, but never to the universal extent we must unhappily recognize in our day. We are no longer in the realm of supposition. We have seen solemn treaties trampled under foot, others shorn of all force in a day; States, *all States*, are seen to fail in their obligations, to repudiate their signatures, to threaten or repay their creditors with the "abhorred vacuum."

We have seen legislators constrained to release individuals themselves from obligations imposed on them by private contracts.

I make so bold as to say—an extraordinary thing!—that gold itself, *gold* is no longer fully possessed of its immemorial and mythical sovereignty; yet once it seemed to contain within its precious and weighty atom the refined essence of confidence! . . .

What we have, then, is a general crisis of values. Nothing escapes, either in the economic or the moral or the political realm. Freedom itself has ceased to be fashionable. Even the most up-to-date opinions, which used to clamor for it furiously fifty years ago, today deny and immolate it! . . . The crisis is spreading to everything: science, civil law, Newton's mechanics, diplomatic traditions. Everything is affected by it. I am not even sure that love itself is not coming to be evaluated in a very different way from that of the last half-dozen centuries. . . .

In short, a crisis of confidence, of fundamental conceptions—there is indeed, a crisis of all human relationships, that is to say, of the values given or received by minds.

But that is not yet all; we must now envisage (and it is with this that I shall end) a crisis of the mind itself. I shall not speak of the particular crisis in the sciences, which seem now to despair of their ancient ideal of explaining the universe as a unified whole. The universe is breaking up, losing all hope of a single design. The world of the ultramicroscopic seems strangely different from the world as an agglomerate mass; in the former, even the identity of bodies is lost. . . . Nor shall I mention the crisis of determinism, that is to say, of causality.

I am thinking, rather, of the dangers that are so seriously threatening the very existence of all the higher values of the mind.

It is clearly possible to conceive an almost happy condition for humanity, or at least a stable, pacified, organized, comfortable condition (I do not say that we are anywhere near it); but in conceiving such a state, we realize that it brings with it, or would bring, a most tepid intellectual temperature: in general, *happy peoples have no mind.* They have no great need of it.

If, then, the world is moving down a certain incline and has already gone some distance down it, we must from now on *recognize that the conditions are rapidly vanishing in which and thanks to which the things we most admire, man's most admirable works so far, have been created and had their influence.*

Everything now conspires against the chances of creating what might be, or rather might have been, noblest and most beautiful. How can this be?

To begin with, it is easy to observe in ourselves a diminution, a kind of general clouding over of sensibility. We moderns are not very sensitive. Modern man has blunted his senses; he puts up with every kind of noise, as we all know; he puts up with nauseating smells, with violently contrasting or insanely intense lighting; he is subjected to perpetual vibration; he feels the need of brutal stimulants, strident sounds, the strongest drinks, brief and bestial emotions.

He tolerates incoherence, he lives in mental disorder. On the other hand, the work of the mind to which we owe everything has become sometimes too facile. Co-ordinated mental effort is today equipped with powerful instruments to make it easier, sometimes to the point of doing away with it. We have invented symbols and built machines to save attention, to relieve us of the patient and difficult labor of the mind; and such methods of symbolization and rapid depiction can only continue to multiply. *Their aim is to do away with the effort of thinking.*

Finally, the conditions of modern life tend inevitably, implacably, to make individuals all alike, to level character; and, unhappily yet necessarily, the average tends to decline *toward the lowest type*. Bad money drives out good.

Another danger: I notice that credulity and naïveté are developing to an alarming degree. I have noticed in the last few years a number of new superstitions that were nonexistent in France twenty years ago and now are gradually coming even into our drawing rooms. We see very distinguished people knocking on wood and practicing other exorcisms and fiduciary acts. Moreover, one of the most striking characteristics of the world today is *futility*: I may say, with no risk of being too harsh, that we are torn between futility and anxiety. We have the finest playthings man has ever possessed: the motorcar, the yo-yo, the radio, and the cinema; we have everything that genius could create for transmitting, with the speed of light, things not always of the highest quality. What amusements—never so many toys! But what anxieties— never so many alarms!

And lastly, what chores! Chores concealed in comfort itself! Chores that from day to day are only multiplied by our efficiency and our concern for the morrow; for we are caught by the ever more perfect organization of life in an ever tighter net of rules and constraints, many of which we never notice! We are by no means aware of all the things we obey. The telephone rings, we hurry to it; the clock strikes, an appointment calls us. . . . Think of the work schedules, the timetables, the growing demands of hygiene, even the standardization of spelling, which used not to exist, even regulated street crossings; and think what they mean in terms of their effect on the mind. . . . Everything commands us, everything puts pressure on us, everything prescribes what we have to do and tells us to do it automatically. Testing our reflexes has become the important test of the day.

Even the fashion industries have put fantasy under discipline, under *regulations* to control copying, whereby the secret schemes of business rule the aesthetics of the day.

In short, in every way we are circumscribed, dominated by a hidden or obvious regimentation extending to everything, and we are so bewildered by the chaos of stimuli obsessing us that *we end by needing it*.

Are these not detestable conditions for the future production of works of art comparable to those which humanity has created in preceding centuries? We have lost the *leisure to ripen*, and if we look into ourselves as artists, we no longer find that other virtue of our predecessors in the creation of beauty: the aim to endure. Of the many beliefs I have said were dying, one is already gone: that is the belief in posterity and its judgment.

We are now at the end of this review of disorder, which has been rapid and perforce without order. Perhaps you are expecting me to draw some conclusion. We like a play to end happily, or at least to end. You shall have prompt satisfaction on the latter point. For the other, I repeat that my subject is precisely the impossibility of concluding. The need for a conclusion is so strong in us that we irresistibly and absurdly import conclusions into history and even into politics. We cut out patterns of events to make well-rounded tragedies; we want a war, when it ends, to have a clear-cut ending. There is no need for me to tell you that unfortunately this desire is illusory. We believe, too, that a revolution is a clear solution, and we know that this is not true either. These are but crude oversimplifications. . . .

The only conclusion to a study of this kind, to this glimpse of chaos, the only conclusion that might be desirable would be a prediction or presentiment of some sort of future. But I abhor prophesying. Some time ago someone came and asked me what I augured of life and what I thought things would be like in fifty years. As I shrugged my shoulders, the questioner lowered his sights and his prices, and said: "Well, where shall we be in twenty years?" I replied: "*We are backing into the future*," and I added: "How much could anyone have foreseen in 1882, or 1892, of what has happened since that time? In 1882, fifty years ago, it was impossible to foresee the events and discoveries that have profoundly transformed the face of the earth." And I added, further: "Sir, in 1892 would you have foreseen that in 1932, in order to cross a street in Paris, you would have to seek the protection of a six-month-old baby—negotiate a street-crossing under the safe-conduct of an infant?" He replied: "No, that is something I shouldn't have foreseen either."

In short, more and more it is becoming useless and even dangerous to make predictions based on evidence from yesterday or the day before; but it is still wise, and this will be my last word, to be ready for anything, or almost anything. We must keep in our minds and hearts the will to lucid understanding and precision of mind, a sense of greatness and risk, a sense of the extraordinary adventure on which mankind has set out, departing perhaps too far from the primary and natural conditions of his species, and headed I know not where!

On History

[1931]

HISTORY is the most dangerous product evolved from the chemistry of the intellect. Its properties are well known. It causes dreams, it intoxicates whole peoples, gives them false memories, quickens their reflexes, keeps their old wounds open, torments them in their repose, leads them into delusions either of grandeur or persecution, and makes nations bitter, arrogant, insufferable, and vain.

History will justify anything. It teaches precisely nothing, for it contains everything and furnishes examples of everything.

How many books have been written entitled "the lesson of this, the teaching of that"! Nothing could make more absurd reading, after the events that actually followed, instead of the ones the books told us would be the way of the future.

In the present state of the world the danger of letting oneself be seduced by history is greater than it ever was.

The political phenomena of our time are accompanied and complicated by an unexampled *change of scale*, or rather by a *change in the order of things*. The world to which we are beginning to belong, both men and nations, is only *similar* to the world that was once familiar to us. The system of causes controlling the fate of every one of us, and now extending over

114

the whole globe, makes it reverberate throughout at every shock; there are no more questions that can be settled by being settled at one point.

History as it was formerly conceived was pictured as a group of parallel chronological tables, between which certain transverse accidentals were sometimes marked here and there. A few attempts at synchronization produced no results, apart from a kind of demonstration of their futility. What was happening at Peking in Caesar's time, or on the Zambezi in Napoleon's time, happened on another planet. But *melodic* history is no longer possible. All political themes are now intermingled, and each event as it occurs immediately takes on a number of simultaneous and inseparable meanings.

The policy of a Richelieu or a Bismarck loses its way and its meaning in these new surroundings. The notions they employed in their schemes, the aims they could propose to the ambition of their peoples, the forces that figured in their calculations, all these have become unimportant. The chief business of politicians was—and still is, for some—*to acquire territory*. Force was applied, the coveted land was taken from someone, and that was that. But who can fail to see that those enterprises which used to be limited to a talk followed by a duel followed by a pact, will in the future inspire such inevitable generalizations as *nothing can ever happen again without the whole world's taking a hand*; that no one will ever be able to predict or circumscribe the almost immediate consequences of any undertaking whatever.

All the genius of the great governments of the past has been exhausted, rendered impotent and even *useless* by the enlarged field and the greater number of connections between political phenomena, for there is no genius, no vigor of character or intellect, no tradition—even the British—that can henceforward pride itself on countering or modifying at will the mood and reactions of a human world in which the old *geometry of history* and the old *mechanics of politics* no longer in the least apply.

Europe makes me think of an object suddenly transported into a more complex space where all its known characteristics, though remaining the same in appearance, are subjected to quite different *relations*. In particular, the forecasts that were possible, the traditional calculations, have become emptier than they ever were.

The aftermath of the recent war* has shown us events that would formerly have determined for a long time, and precisely *in the direction they indicated*, the shape and progress of general policy; but now, after a few years and in consequence of the number of parties engaged, the enlargement of the theater and the complication of interests, those events are deprived of their energy and absorbed or contradicted by their immediate consequences.

We must expect such transformations to become the rule. The farther we go the less simple and predictable the effects will be, and the less any political operations and even interventions of force—in a word, obvious and direct action—will turn out as they were expected to do. *The sizes, areas, and masses involved, their relations, the impossibility of localizing anything, the prompt repercussions, all will more and more impose a policy very different from the existing one.*

Effects are so rapidly becoming incalculable from their causes, and even contradictory to their causes, that henceforward it will perhaps be thought puerile, dangerous, and senseless to look for the causal event, to try to produce it or prevent it; perhaps the political mind will stop thinking in

* That of 1914–18. [P.V.]

terms of events, a habit that is essentially due to history and sustained by it. It is not that there will be no more events and even "monumental moments" in time; there will be immense ones! But those whose function it is to anticipate them, to prepare for them or against them, will necessarily learn more and more to be wary of their sequel. It will not be enough to have both desire and ability to engage in an undertaking. Nothing was more completely ruined by the last war than the pretension to foresight. But it was not from any lack of knowledge of history, surely?

Historical Fact

[1932]

My Young Friends,
FIRST of all let me tell you about a memory of a memory. The remarkable and thoughtful address we have just heard reminded me of a little scene once described for me by the great painter Degas.

He told me that when he was a small child his mother took him one day to the Rue de Tournon to visit Mme Le Bas, widow of the famous Member of the Convention, who shot himself on the Ninth Thermidor.

The visit over, they were slowly making their way to the front door, accompanied by the old lady, when Mme Degas suddenly halted, strongly moved. Dropping her son's hand, she pointed to the portraits of Robespierre, Couthon, and Saint-Just which she had just recognized on the walls of the vestibule, and she could not help exclaiming in horror: "What! Do you still keep those monsters' faces here!" "Hush, Célestine!" Mme Le Bas replied warmly. "Hush! They were saints!"

And that, my dear young people, may be easily related to what M. Lanson was telling us. In a few words, Professor Lanson has put before you in a most striking manner the contrasting opinions of several historians of the first rank, concerning the men and events of the French Revolution.

He has shown you that those experts on the Terror agreed with each other precisely as Danton agreed with Robespierre —although with less extreme consequences. I do not say that the impulses of the mind are one bit less positive in writers than in men of action, but in normal times the guillotine, luckily, is not at the disposal of historians.

Yet I shall not conceal from you that if the deeper meaning of philosophical quarrels and even literary polemics were looked into, traced back to the heart by some relentless analysis, there is no doubt that we should find at the root of our opinions and our favorite theories some strange source of implacable determination, some obscure blind will *to be right* by exterminating the enemy. Convictions are simply and secretly murderous.

You have seen, then, in the quotations and the precise comments brought together for you, how different minds proceeding from the same data, bringing to bear on the same documents their critical powers and their talents for imaginative organization—and moreover animated (I trust) by an identical desire to reach the truth—are yet divided and opposed, repelling each other almost as violently as political factions.

Whether historians or partisans, men of learning or men of action, they make themselves—half-consciously, half-unconsciously—infinitely sensitive to certain facts or certain characteristics, and completely insensitive to others, which would hamper or destroy their theories; and neither the degree of cultivation of their minds, nor the solidity and amplitude of their knowledge, nor even their loyalty, nor their profundity seems to have the slightest influence on what might be called their *capacity for historical dissent*.

Whether we listen to Mme Degas or to Mme Le Bas, or

to the noble, pure, and gentle severity of Joseph de Maistre; or to the great, fiery Michelet; or to Taine, or Tocqueville, or to M. Aulard or M. Mathiez . . . there are as many opinions as persons, as many points of view as pairs of eyes. Every historian of that tragic period holds out to us some severed head as the object of his partiality.

What could be more remarkable than that such dissensions should persist, in spite of the quantity and quality of the work done on the same remnants of the past; and that they should even get worse, and that minds should grow more hardened and divergent, in that very work which ought to lead them to the same conclusions?

In vain do we increase our efforts, vary our methods, broaden or limit the field of study, examine things from a distance, or probe the microscopic structure of an epoch, ransack personal archives, family papers, private records, contemporary newspapers, municipal decrees; these various developments do not converge, they find no single idea as their limit. The final term of each is the nature and character of their authors, and only one proof ever results from them, which is the impossibility of separating the observer from the thing observed, and history from the historian.

There are, however, points on which everybody agrees. In every history book there are certain propositions on which the actors, witnesses, historians, and factions are united. These are strokes of luck, true *accidents*; and it is these accidents, these remarkable exceptions all taken together, that constitute the unquestionable part of our knowledge of the past. These accidents of agreement, these coincidences of consent define "historical facts"—but not entirely.

Everyone agrees that Louis XIV died in 1715. But in 1715 an infinite number of other observable things occurred which

120

would require an infinite number of words, books, and even libraries if they were to be preserved in written form. We must therefore *choose*, that is, agree not only on the *existence* but also on the *importance* of the fact; and the latter is capital. Agreement on existence means that men can *believe* only what seems to them least tainted with humanity, and that they consider complete agreement so unlikely that it justifies eliminating their personalities, their instincts, their interests, their individual vision—all of them sources of error and potential falsification. But since we cannot retain everything, and since we have to free ourselves from the infinitude of facts by judging their relative interest for the future, the decision on importance inevitably reintroduces into the historical work the very thing we had just tried to eliminate. As your classmates in Philosophy would say, importance is completely subjective. Importance is a matter of discretion, as is the value of testimony. One may reasonably think the discovery of the properties of Peruvian bark more *important* than such and such a treaty concluded at about the same time; and, indeed, today in 1932 the consequences of this diplomatic instrument may be totally lost and, as it were, diffused in the chaos of events, whereas fever is still with us, the marshy regions of the globe are being increasingly inhabited and exploited, and quinine has perhaps been indispensable to the exploration and settlement of the whole earth, which is, *to my mind*, the dominant fact of our century.

You see, I too am making my own criteria of importance.

Besides, history demands and implies many other biases. For example, among the rules of the game there is one that is so readily thought to be significant in itself and capable of use without precaution that I caused a scandal some time ago by trying to find the exact expression for it.

Do I dare speak to you of *dates*, which once so cruelly ruled over every examination? Do I dare disturb your youthful notion of causality, by reminding you of that old sophistry, *post hoc ergo propter hoc*, which plays so great a part in history? Shall I tell you that the numerical sequence of dates has the same great but limited value as the order of the alphabet and that, moreover, the succession of events, or their coincidence, has no meaning except in each particular case and within the limited area where those events may, *from the point of view of some witness*, act or react one on another? I should be afraid of astonishing and shocking you if I insinuated that Micromegas, were he to wander at random in Time and fall from ancient Alexandria at the height of its glory into an African village or some hamlet in France today, would necessarily suppose that the brilliant capital of the Ptolemies was three or four thousand years *later* than the agglomeration of huts or hovels whose inhabitants are our contemporaries.

All such assumptions are inevitable. I am criticizing only our negligence in not making them explicit, conscious, palpable to the mind. I regret that no one has yet done for history what the exact sciences did for themselves when they revised their fundamentals, searching with the greatest care for their axioms and numbering their postulates.

This is perhaps because History is above all a *Muse*, and we prefer that she should be so. At this point I can say no more. . . . I honor the Muses.

It is also because the *past* is an entirely mental thing. It is nothing but images and beliefs. Notice that we use a kind of contradictory procedure for evoking the various figures of the different epochs. On the one hand, we need the free use of our ability to pretend, to live other lives than our own; on the other, we must restrain that freedom in order to take account of documents; and we make an effort to arrange and organize past events by using our own energy and our own forms of thought and attention, things *essentially of the present*. You can observe this in yourselves: every time you are overtaken by history and think historically, every time you allow yourself to be inveigled into reliving the human adventure of some past era, your interest in it is wholly sustained by your feeling that things could have happened entirely otherwise, could have taken quite a different turn. At each moment you imagine a *next moment* unlike the one that actually followed: that is, for each imaginary present in which you place yourself, you conceive a different future from the one that actually took place.

IF Robespierre had won?—IF Grouchy had arrived in time on the field of Waterloo?—IF Napoleon had had Louis XVI's navy and a man like Suffren . . . IF . . . always IF.

This little conjunction *if* is full of meaning. In itself, perhaps, it holds the secret of the most intimate link between life and history. It imparts to the study of the past the anxiety and expectation that define the present. It confers on history the power of novels and tales. It allows us to share in that suspense in the face of uncertainty which is the principal sensation of great lives, of nations in battle when their fate is at stake, of ambitious men when they see that the next moment will mean the crown or the scaffold, of the artist about to unveil his statue or order the removal of the trusses and props that still support his building. . . .

If this element of living time were removed from history, we should find that its very substance—*pure* history, history composed of *facts* only, those incontestable facts that I have mentioned—is quite pointless, for facts by themselves have no meaning. From time to time, someone says to you: "This is a fact. You must bow before the fact." What he is saying is: "You must *believe* . . . you must believe because man has had nothing to do with it. It is things themselves speaking. *It is a fact.*"

Yes. But what is to be done with a *fact*? More than anything else, a fact is like the Pythian oracles or those royal dreams that Joseph and Daniel, in the Bible, interpret for their terrified kings. In history, as in everything else, what is positive is ambiguous. What is real lends itself to an infinite number of interpretations.

That is why De Maistre and Michelet are both possible; and that is why, perhaps, when they speculate on the past they become oracles, augurs, prophets, adopting the same grandeur of style and the same sublimity of language, while they confer on the past all the living profundity that in truth belongs only to the future.

And so, within ourselves, looking backward and looking forward, grasping the past or sensing the future are much the same thing, for we cannot help oscillating between images; and our perpetual present is like an interval between equidistant suppositions, one assuming the past and the other presuming a future.

You young people now before me make me dream of times I shall never see, as well as those I shall see no more. I look at you and see myself at your age, and am tempted to foresee.

I have been talking to you far too long about history, and nearly forgot to tell you the essential thing, which is this: the best way to get an idea of the value and use of history—the best way of learning to read it and use it—consists in taking one's own experience as typical of all knowledge of past events, in drawing from the present the model for our curiosity about the past. What we have seen with our own eyes, what we have personally experienced, what we were and what we did—these should provide us with the questionnaire, drawn from our own life; we shall then ask history to fill it out, and she must do her best to answer when we ask her about times we never lived through. *What was it like to live in such and such a period?* That, at bottom, is the whole question. All the abstractions and notions you find in books are empty if you are not given the means of discovering them in your own experience.

But when we look at ourselves historically—*sub specie historiae*—we are led to a certain problem; and its solution will immediately affect our judgment of the value of history. If history is anything more than a diversion for the mind, it is because we hope to draw lessons from it. We think we can deduce from knowledge of the past some foreknowledge of the future.

Let us now match this pretension with our personal history; and if we are already several decades old, let us try to compare what has happened with what we expected—the event with the anticipation.

I was in Rhetoric Class in 1887. (Rhetoric has since become the First Form or Senior Class: a great change, which could give us much to reflect on.)

Well, I now ask myself how much of what has since happened could be foreseen in 1887—forty-five years ago?

Note that we have the very best conditions for historical experience. We have at our disposal perhaps an excessive quantity of data: books, newspapers, photographs, personal recollections, and numerous eyewitnesses. History has not generally been put together out of such a wealth of materials.

So, what could be foreseen? I merely pose the problem.

And I shall point out no more than a few features of the time when I was doing my Rhetoric.

In those days, we saw in the streets a great many animals hardly ever seen nowadays except on racecourses, and not a single automobile. (Let us note here that according to certain scholars the use of the horse for traction did not become widespread until the thirteenth century, thus freeing Europe from porterage, a system requiring slaves. This comparison allows you to conceive of the motorcar as an "historical fact.")

In 1887, too, the air was strictly reserved for real birds. Electricity had not yet lost its wires. Solid bodies were still fairly solid. Opaque bodies were still quite opaque. Newton and Galileo reigned in peace. Physics was happy and its references absolute. Time flowed by in quiet days: all hours were equal in the sight of the Universe. Space enjoyed being infinite, homogeneous, and perfectly indifferent to what went on in its august bosom. Matter felt that it had good and just laws and did not suspect for a moment that in the realm of the ultramicroscopic certain of them could change, to the point of losing in that abyss of division the very sense of law.

All this is now but dreams and smoke. All this has been transformed like the map of Europe, like the political face of the planet, like the appearance of our streets, or like my own schoolfellows—those who are still alive—who, when I last saw them, were students more or less, and who are now senators, generals, deans, presidents, or members of the Institute.

The latter transformations might have been foreseen, but what of the others? Could the greatest scholar, the profoundest philosopher, the most calculating politician of 1887 even have dreamed of what we now see, after a mere forty-five years? We cannot even conceive what operations of the mind, dealing with the historical material accumulated in 1887, could have deduced from even the most informed knowledge of the past, even a crudely approximate idea of what exists in 1932.

That is why I shall take care not to prophesy. I feel too keenly, and I have said so elsewhere, that *we are backing into the future.* That, for me, is the surest and most important lesson of history, for history is the science of things that do not repeat themselves. Things that repeat themselves, experiments that can be performed again, observations that are identical, belong to physics, and to some extent to biology.

Yet I would not have you think it fruitless to meditate on the past in its pastness. In particular it shows us the frequent failure of predictions that are too precise, and, on the other hand, the great advantages of a general and constant *preparation* which—without claiming to determine or defy events, for these are invariably surprising or develop surprising consequences—makes it possible for men to maneuver readily against the unexpected.

You young people are starting out in life, and you will find yourselves involved in a very interesting period. An interesting period is always an enigmatic one, promising little repose, prosperity, continuity, or security. We live in a critical age, that is to say an age in which a number of incompatible things are found together, none of which can either vanish or prevail. This state of things is so complex and so new that no one today can boast of understanding it—which does not mean that no one does so boast. All the notions we thought solid, all the values of civilized life, all that made for stability in international relations, all that made for regularity in the economy . . . in a word, all that tended happily to limit the uncertainty of the morrow, all that gave to nations and individuals some confidence in the morrow . . . all this seems badly compromised. I have consulted all the augurs I could find, of every species, and I have heard only vague words, contradictory prophecies, curiously feeble assurances. Never has humanity combined so much power with so much disorder, so much anxiety with so many playthings, so much knowledge with so much uncertainty. Worry and futility divide our days between them.

It is for you now, my dear young people, to make a start in life, and shortly in your work. There is no lack of tasks. In arts, letters, science, in practical affairs, in politics, you can and you should consider that everything is to be rethought and redone. You will have to count on yourselves far more than we had to. You must therefore equip your minds, which does not mean that learning is enough. There is no point in possessing what you have no intention of using, thus making it part of your thought. It is with knowledge as with words. A limited vocabulary, but one with which you can make numerous combinations, is better than thirty thousand words that only hamper the action of the mind. I am not going to offer you advice. Advice should be given to the very elderly, and the young often do so. Allow me, however, to ask you to listen to one or two further remarks.

Modern life tends to spare us intellectual effort just as it does physical effort. For example, it replaces imagination by images, reasoning by symbols and writing, or by machines . . . and often by nothing. It offers us every facility, every *short cut* for arriving at our goal without making the journey. And this is excellent, but it is also rather dangerous. It combines with other causes, which I shall not enumerate, to produce— how shall I put it—a certain general diminution of value and effort in the realm of the mind. I wish I were wrong; but my

128

own observation is unfortunately confirmed by others. When machines reduced the necessity of physical effort, athletics fortunately came along to save and even to glorify the muscular man. We should perhaps consider the utility of doing for the mind what has been done for the body. I dare not tell you that everything that requires no effort is a waste of time. But there are a few atoms of truth in that cruel sentence.

Here at last is my final word: history, I fear, scarcely enables us to foresee; but combined with independence of mind, it can help us to see. Look at the world today, and then look at France. Her situation is singular; she is fairly strong, and is regarded with no very friendly eye. It is important that she should count on herself alone. Here it is that history intervenes to teach us that our internal quarrels have always been fatal to us. When France feels united, nothing avails against her.

The Outlook for Intelligence

[1935]

A LITTLE over two years ago, in this same place, I had the honor to speak on what I called "Politics of the Mind." You may remember that under this title (which is not exactly clear) I was concerned over the present state of things in the world, and was inquiring into the facts of which we are the witnesses and agents, dealing not so much with their political or economic character as with the situation they have created for affairs of the mind. I dwelt (perhaps at too great length) on this critical situation, and I said, in effect, that a disorder to which no end could be imagined was observable on every hand. We find it around us and within us, in our daily habits, in our manners, in the newspapers, in our pleasures, and even in our knowledge. Interruption, incoherence, surprise are the ordinary conditions of our life. They have even become real needs for many people, whose minds are no longer fed, it would seem, by anything but sudden changes and constantly renewed stimuli. The words "sensational," "amazing," commonly used today, are the kind of words that describe an era. We can no longer bear anything that lasts. We no longer know how to make boredom bear fruit. Our nature abhors a vacuum, any kind of empty space on which, in the past, minds knew how to project the image of their ideals—their Ideas, in Plato's sense. This state of things, which I called "chaotic," is the combined result of the works and the accumulated labor of men. Of course it points to some kind of future, but one that is absolutely impossible for us to imagine; and among many other innovations, *this* is one of the greatest. We can no longer deduce from what we know any notion of the future to which we can give the slightest credence.

Within a few decades, in fact, we have destroyed and created so much, at the expense of the past—refuting and disorganizing it, reorganizing the ideas, methods, and institutions it had bequeathed us—that the present seems without precedent or example. We no longer look on the past as a son looks on his father, from whom he may learn something, but as a grown man looks on a child. . . . At times we might even fancy reviving the greatest of our ancestors for the pleasure of instructing and astonishing them.

I often find amusement in imagining the resurrection of one of our great men of the past. I offer to be his guide and walk with him through Paris; I listen as he presses me with questions, or exclaims with wonder. By such childish means, I force myself to feel astonished at what I see every day without astonishment, and so feel the immense difference which the passage of time has made between life in the past and life today. But I soon feel helpless in my role as a guide. Just imagine all you would need to know if you had to explain to some resurrected Descartes or Napoleon our present way of life, to make him understand how we can manage to live in such strange conditions, in surroundings he would surely find rather frightening and even hostile. My helplessness is a measure of the change that has taken place.

I can here touch only lightly on the enormous question of the changes, beyond all foreseeing, which have so profoundly transformed the world and, in a mere few years, made it unrecognizable to any observer who has lived long enough to have seen it otherwise. I must stress the short time it has taken to bring about such tremendous changes, and above all I would have your minds dwell a little on the causes that have been most powerful in this sudden mutation. I am thinking of all the new facts, entirely new, prodigiously new facts that have come to light since the beginning of the last century.

Before that time, scientific research had dealt only with well-known phenomena—that is, phenomena that had been *perceptible since the beginning of time, and, moreover, directly perceptible*. Of course, the notion of the universe had been changing profoundly, and so had the notion of science itself, correlatively; but the quantity of observable phenomena on the one hand, and man's powers of action on the other, had not perceptibly increased. Now, in 1800, I think, the discovery of the electric current, by means of that admirable invention the battery, opened up the era of new facts that were to change the face of the world. It is not without interest to pause at that date; to reflect that it is only a hundred and thirty-five years ago that this revelation took place. You know its wonderful sequel: how the whole field of electrodynamics and electromagnetism was opened up to the passionate curiosity of scientists, how its applications have multiplied, how the relations between electricity and light were discovered, with all the consequences in theory that followed; and finally, radiation, the study of which has called into question all our physical knowledge and even our habits of thought.

Now think how many are the radically new and unpredictable facts that in less than a century and a half have startled our minds, from the electric current to X rays and the various forms of radiation discovered since Curie; add to these the many practical applications, from telegraph to television, and you will understand by reflecting on this absolutely new thing that has come into the world of man in so short a time (and whose possibilities seem limitless) *what an effort of adaptation is required of our race, limited for so long to considering and using phenomena that had been accessible to firsthand observation from the beginning.*

I shall now tell you a little story to underline the idea I am proposing, which is, in short, that the human race is entering a phase of its history in which all prediction becomes—by the sheer fact of being a prediction—a risk of error, a suspect product of our minds.

Imagine, then, that all the greatest scientists down to about the end of the eighteenth century—the Archimedes, the Newtons, the Galileos, and the Descartes—are gathered in some part of the lower world, and a messenger from earth brings a dynamo for them to examine at their leisure. They are told that this apparatus is used by the living to produce movement, light, or heat. They look at it, they set it going. Next, they take it to pieces, and inspect and measure each part. In short, they do all they can. . . . But they know nothing about the electric current, they know nothing about induction, they only know about mechanical transformation. "What are those coiled wires for?" they ask. They are forced to recognize their incompetence. So, all knowledge and all human genius, united in the face of this mysterious object, fail to discover its secret, fail to guess the new fact established by Volta, and other facts discovered by Ampère, Faraday, et al. . . .

(We must not fail to notice here that all those great men

who have just shown themselves incapable of understanding a dynamo fallen from earth to the lower world, have done exactly what we do when we inspect a brain, weigh it, dissect it, cut it into thin slices and submit these prepared sections to histological examination. Our natural transformer remains incomprehensible to us. . . .)

Notice, too, that for my story about the dynamo, I have chosen minds of the first magnitude, reduced to incompetence by their radical inability to explain an apparatus whose operation and use are today familiar to so many and have even become indispensable to the life of society.

In short, we have the privilege—or the truly interesting misfortune—of witnessing a profound, rapid, and irresistible transformation of all the conditions of human action.

You should by no means imagine that our predecessors could have witnessed such obvious and extraordinary changes during their own lives. Some forty years ago, a friend of mine, in my presence, was making light of the well-known expression "period of transition," and said it was an absurd cliché. "Every period is a transition," he said. At that point I picked up a piece of sugar (the conversation occurred after dinner), showed it to him, put it in my cup of coffee, and said:

"Do you imagine this lump of sugar, which has been in the sugar bowl for quite a long time, and quite at peace, is not in the process of experiencing sensations of an entirely novel kind? Is it not, at the moment, in a period which it might call 'transitional'? Do you imagine that a woman expecting a child does not feel in quite a different state than before, and that she cannot call this part of her life a period of transition? I hope she can, both for her sake and the child's."

And today I say:

"Do you imagine that a man who lived through the years

134

from 1872 to 1890, for example, and then from the years 1890 to 1935, would not feel some difference of rhythm between these two periods of his life?"

I do not wish to recount all that has been profoundly modified, altered, and replaced in the last thirty years—having shown you the essentials of that picture of transformation two years ago. I shall simply say, by way of summarizing my thought and introducing the subject I shall deal with today, that some thirty years ago it was still possible to examine the things of the world *in historical perspective*; that is, everyone in those days expected to find in the present (the present of those days) a fairly intelligible sequel and development of the events that had taken place in the past. Continuity reigned in their minds. With no great difficulty, models, examples, precedents, and causes could be found in documents, memoirs, and historical works. This was general; and apart from a few innovations of an industrial order, the rest of what made up civilization was quite easily linked with the past. But during the thirty or forty years we have just lived through, there have been too many innovations in every field. There have been too many surprises, too many things created or destroyed; and too many great and sudden developments have brutally inter-rupted the intellectual tradition—that continuity I spoke of. More and more numerous problems every day, perfectly new and unexpected problems have arisen on all sides, in politics, in the arts, in science. In all human affairs, all the cards have been reshuffled. *Man is now assailed by questions that no man before had imagined*, whether philosopher, scientist, or layman; everyone has somehow been taken unawares. *Every man belongs to two eras.*

In the past, the rare innovations that occurred were merely

solutions or answers to problems or questions that were ancient if not immemorial. But our kind of innovation consists, not in the answers, but in the true novelty of the questions themselves; in the statement of problems, not in their solution.

Hence that general sense of helplessness and incoherence that pervades our minds, keeping us on the alert, in a state of anxiety to which we can neither become accustomed nor foresee any end. On one hand is the past that can neither be abolished nor forgotten, but from which we can derive almost nothing that will orient us in the present or help us to imagine the future. On the other hand, there is the future without the least shape. Every day we are at the mercy of some invention, some accident, either practical or intellectual.

One has merely to look back at a pile of newspapers a few months old to see how consistently events can, in a few days, confound the prognostications of the most competent men. Must I go so far as to add that a competent man is coming to be a man who makes mistakes, and does so while obeying all the rules? I cannot help thinking of that brain trust that was organized in America and, after a few weeks, broke up, still arguing.

On all hands, all over the world, in every field of endeavor, we can see nothing but projects, plans, experiments, tests, and tryouts, all of them hasty.

Russia, Germany, Italy, the United States are like vast laboratories in which research proceeds on a hitherto unknown scale; where the attempt is being made to fashion a new man, to give us a new economy, new manners, a new life, even new religions. And the same is true in the sciences, the arts, in all human affairs.

But, confronted as we are with a situation at once so agonizing and so stimulating, the question of human intelligence itself arises; the mind is faced with the whole question of intelligence—its limits, its preservation, its probable future —and for the mind this is the paramount question of the day.

In fact, the disorder I spoke of and the difficulties we are now considering are simply the obvious consequences of the intense intellectual development that has transformed the world. The origin of this crisis is a matter of labor and capital—the capital of ideas and knowledge, and the labor of minds. What we can easily discover at the root of the economic and political phenomena of our time are thought, research, argument—the intellectual labors. A single example: the introduction of hygiene into Japan has caused the population of that empire to double in thirty-five years! ... A few notions have built up, in a mere thirty-five years, an enormous political pressure.

So the mind, functioning furiously and as though on the blindest impulse, producing implements of great power, has brought about tremendous events, on a world-wide scale; and this transformation of the human world has taken place in no order, on no pre-established plan, and above all without regard to human nature—the slow pace of its adaptation and evolution, and its fundamental limitations. It may be said that *everything we know*, which is to say, *everything we can do*, has finally been turned against *what we are*.

And now we are faced with a question: we need to know whether this world, prodigiously transformed but also terribly shaken up by so much power so imprudently applied, can now take on a rational order, can quickly return to, or rather quickly arrive at, a bearable state of equilibrium. In other words, can the mind get us out of the plight it has got us into? (Notice that the word "rational" which I used just now is, after all, equivalent to the word "quickly"; for an equilibrium is bound to return, as it did after the fall of the Roman Empire, but that took several centuries. And it was brought back by events; whereas the question I am putting is whether the mind itself, acting directly and immediately, can *rationally*, that is, *quickly*, bring back a certain equilibrium within a few years.)

So the whole question comes down to this: can the human mind master what the human mind has made? Can the human intellect save both the world and itself? My object, then, is a kind of examination of the mind's current value and its future or probable value; that is the problem I have set for myself—and shall not solve.

No! You must not imagine that I can even think of solving it: there is no question of that. I cannot pretend even to state it for you completely, or clearly, or simply. The more this question has grown in my mind, the more complex I have seen that it is. But without trying to simplify what is the opposite of simple, or to clarify a thing whose very function is to clarify and which is in itself so obscure, I do mean to give you a sense of the question itself; and to do this, it will be enough, I hope, to show the way in which modern life, the life of most men, affects their minds—influences, stimulates, or wearies them. I say that modern life affects the mind in such a way that we may reasonably feel great anxiety for the survival of intellectual values.

The working conditions of the mind have, in fact, suffered the same fate as all other human affairs, that is to say, they share in the intensity, the haste, the general acceleration of exchanges, as they do in all the consequences of the incoherence, the fantastic flickering of events. I confess that I am so frightened by certain symptoms of degeneration and debility which I observe (or think I observe) in the general trend of intellectual production and consumption, that I sometimes despair of the future! I am sorry to say that I sometimes dream that man's intelligence, and all else by which he deviates from the animal, might one day fail and humanity insensibly return to an instinctive condition, to the uncertainty and futility of the ape. The mind might gradually succumb to the same indifference, inattention, and instability that many things in the present world, in its tastes, manners, and ambitions, either display already or give us cause to dread. And I say to myself (without believing it):

"All human history, insofar as it is a manifestation of thought, will perhaps have been merely the result of a sort of crisis, an aberrant growth, like one of those sudden mutations to be observed in Nature, which disappear as oddly as they came. There have been unstable species, monstrosities of size, power, and unwieldiness, that have not endured. Who knows if all our culture is not a hypertrophy, a 'sport,' an untenable development, which a few hundred centuries will have sufficed to bring into being and to an end?"

This is doubtless a very exaggerated notion, and I express it here only to give you a sense, in a few rough strokes, of just how far one may be preoccupied with the fate of the intellect. Yet it is only too easy to justify such fears. All that is needed to show you the real seed from which they spring is to point out a few of the dark spots on the horizon of the mind.

Let us begin by examining the faculty which is fundamental, which is mistakenly contrasted with the intelligence, but which is actually its real motive power; I mean the sensibility. If the sensibility of modern man is greatly compromised by the present conditions of his life, and if the future seems to promise an ever harsher treatment, we may be justified in thinking that our intelligence will suffer profoundly from the damage done to our sensibility. But how is the damage being done?

Our modern world is completely occupied with the increasingly thorough and effective exploitation of natural energies. Not only do we seek them and use them to satisfy the eternal necessities of life, but we use them to excess, and are so stimulated by our excess that we create entirely new needs (and some that no one would ever have imagined), out of the very means intended to satisfy these needs, which were nonexistent before. In our present state of industrial civilization, it is as though having invented some substance, we should also, on the basis of its properties, invent an illness to be cured by it, a thirst to be appeased, a pain to be killed. So, for purposes of gain, we are inoculated with tastes and desires that have no roots in our deep physiological life but rather result from psychic or sensory stimuli deliberately inflicted. Modern man is drunk on waste—too much speed, too much light, too many tonics, stimulants, drugs . . . too frequent sensations, too much variety, too many echoes, too many facilities, too many wonders, too many of those incredible push buttons that put tremendous consequences within reach of a child's finger. All contemporary life is inseparable from these excesses. Our organism, subjected more and more to constantly new physical and chemical experiments, reacts to the forces and rhythms inflicted on it almost as it would to an *insidious poison*. It gets used to its poison, and soon craves it. Every day it finds the dose too little.

In Ronsard's time, the eye was content with a candle, or even a wick soaked in oil. The scholars of that age, who liked to work at night, could read—and what scrawls!—or write

140

with no trouble at all by a feeble, flickering light. Today, the eye calls for twenty, fifty, a hundred candlepower. The ear requires all the powers of the orchestra, tolerates the wildest dissonances, gets used to the thunder of trucks, the whistling, grinding, and throbbing of machines, and sometimes even wants to hear them in concert music.

As for the most central of our senses, our inner sense of the interval between desire and possession, which is no other than the sense of duration, that feeling of time which was formerly satisfied by the speed of horses, now finds that the fastest trains are too slow, and we fret with impatience between telegrams.

We crave events themselves like food that can never be highly seasoned enough. If every morning there is no great disaster in the world we feel a certain emptiness: "There is nothing in the papers today," we say. We are caught red-handed. We are all poisoned. So I have grounds for saying that there is such a thing as our being intoxicated by energy, just as we are intoxicated by haste, or by size.

Children think a ship is never big enough, a car or an airplane never fast enough; and the idea of the absolute superiority of quantitative greatness, an idea whose naïveté and crudeness are obvious (I hope), is one of the most characteristic ideas of modern man. If we inquire how the mania for haste (for example) affects the powers of the mind, we can easily discover, around us and within us, all the risks of intoxication.

About forty years ago, I pointed out as a critical phenomenon in the history of the world the disappearance of free land; that is to say, all the free territories were finally occupied by organized nations, which meant the end of property belonging to no one. But it may be remarked that, in accord with this political phenomenon, free time also vanished. Free space and free time are now mere memories. The free time I have in mind is not leisure as generally understood. Apparent leisure is still with us, and indeed is protected and propagated by legal measures and mechanical progress, to keep activity from encroaching on free time. Working days are measured and their hours counted by law. But I say that our inner leisure, which is something quite different from chronometric leisure, is being lost. We are losing that essential peace in the depths of our being, that priceless absence in which the most delicate elements of life are refreshed and comforted, while the inner creature is in some way cleansed of past and future, of present awareness, of obligations pending and expectations lying in wait. . . . No cares, no tomorrow, no inner pressure, but a kind of repose in absence, a beneficent emptiness that brings the mind back to its true freedom. Here it is concerned only with itself. Freed from its obligations toward practical knowledge, and unburdened of any care for things to come, it creates forms as pure as crystal. But the demands, the tension, the haste of modern existence disturb or destroy this precious repose. Look within and about you! The progress of insomnia is remarkable, and keeps pace with all other progress. How many people in the world now sleep a synthetic sleep only, and get their supply of oblivion from the skilled industry of organic chemistry! It may be that some new combination of more or less barbituric molecules will bring us meditation too, which life more and more deprives us of in its natural forms. Some day the pharmacopoeia will provide us with profundity as well. But, meanwhile, mental confusion and fatigue are sometimes so great that we take to sighing naïvely for the Tahitis, the paradises of simplicity and idleness, and the slow, vague lives we have never known. Primitive men do not know the necessity of fine divisions of time.

There were no minutes or seconds for the ancients. Artists like Stevenson or Gauguin fled from Europe and reached the islands where there were no clocks. Neither the postman nor the telephone harassed Plato. Virgil never hurried to catch a train. Descartes lost himself in thought on the quays of Amsterdam. But our movements today are regulated by exact fractions of time. Even the twentieth part of a second is beginning to be no longer negligible in certain technical fields.

Doubtless our organism is wonderfully resilient. It has so far stood up under this more and more inhuman treatment but, after all, will it forever tolerate such constraint, such excesses? That is not all. God knows how much we endure, how much our unhappy sensibility must compensate for as best it can!

. . . .

Faced with all these facts, I am not far from concluding that sensibility in modern man is being debased. A stronger stimulus, a greater expense of energy are needed for us to feel anything, which means that the delicacy of our senses, after a period of refinement, is diminishing. I am sure that a precise measurement of the energy required today by the senses of civilized men would show that the thresholds of our sensibility are getting higher—that is, sensibility itself is becoming more obtuse.

This dulling of sensibility is strongly indicated by our grow-ing general indifference to ugliness and brutal sights.

We have developed our museums with a view to cultiva-tion in art. We have introduced a kind of aesthetic education into our schools. But these are specious measures that can only end in spreading an abstract erudition having no real effect. It is simply a matter of distributing a kind of learning with no living depth; we go on allowing our highways, streets, and squares to be disgraced by monuments that are an offense to the eye and the mind, our cities to grow in disorder, our State or private buildings to be built without the slightest regard for the simplest requirements of a feeling for form.

But I am here bordering on the realm of ethics. Our decadence as regards the disposition of buildings and perspectives comes, in great part, from the exaggerated mania for regulations, which is itself a symptom of degeneration in our sense of responsibility.

All city planning and construction should proceed from definite, voluntary action. These are matters of art. They should therefore not result from the deliberations of a council, a committee, a commission, or any constituted body whatever, however well composed. To build is to give reality to a certain desire of the eye, a desire that must gradually be defined and analyzed by the mind, and so brought closer to its realization in action and material. But one of the signs of the failure of character in our time is the subordination of action to regulation and the general prevalence of distrust and group discussion.

I shall come back to this presently.

But let us now consider one of the chief objects of our inquiry, perhaps the most important.

The whole future of intelligence depends on education, or rather on the training, of every kind, received by the mind. The terms education and training must not here be taken in a restricted sense. When we hear them used, we generally think of the systematic instruction of children and adolescents by parents or teachers. But let us not forget that our entire life may be considered as an education, no longer organized or even organizable, but, on the contrary, essentially disorderly, consisting of the whole lot of impressions and acquisitions, good or bad, that come to us from life itself. School is not the only instructor of youth. Their surroundings and the age itself have as much influence on them as their teachers, and more. The streets, the shows, what they hear, the company they keep, the general climate of the times, changing fashions (and by fashions I mean not only those in dress and manners but those to be observed also in language), have a powerful and constant influence on their minds.

But let us first turn our attention to organized education, the kind dogmatically dispensed in schools. I shall make a preliminary remark which I believe is called for by the most obvious characteristic of our time. I presume that we can no longer deal with any question regarding human life without taking into account the different forms it assumes throughout the civilized world. In all matters, our age requires of us, or imposes on us, a wider view than ever before. The study of a human problem can no longer be limited to what goes on in one particular nation. Our investigation must be extended to neighboring or sometimes very distant peoples. Human relations have become so immediate and so numerous, and repercussions so rapid and often so surprising, that an inquiry into every order of phenomena found within a limited area is not enough to inform us of the conditions and possibilities of life, even the local conditions and possibilities in that one locality. All knowledge today is necessarily comparative knowledge.

Now the men of tomorrow in Europe, that is, the children and young people of today, are divided into very different groups. And tomorrow these groups will find themselves face to face—in competition or collaboration or antagonism. We would do well, therefore, to compare what we are doing for our children with what other nations are doing for theirs; and we must think of the possible consequences of such dissimilar types of education. I shall not stress this. But I cannot help reminding you that, in three or four great countries, the whole of their youth have for some years been subjected to a process of education essentially political in character. *Politics first* is the rule in the school programs and disciplines of those nations. Their programs and disciplines are calculated to produce uniformity in young minds; and to that end certain remarkably precise political and social aims outweigh all considerations of culture. The smallest details of school life, the inculcation of manners, the games, the books available to young people, everything must work together to turn them into men who will fit into a social structure and adapt themselves to perfectly definite social or national goals. Freedom of the mind is strictly subordinated to State doctrine, whose principles, of course, vary from one nation to another, but whose goal of uniformity is everywhere the same. *The State shapes men to its own ends.*

Our own young people, then, will soon find themselves confronted with several groups of homogeneous youth who have been molded, trained, and, so to speak, *nationalized*. A modern State of this type tolerates no nonconformity in education; and education, beginning at the tenderest age, will not let its victim go, but prolongs and perfects his training in postgraduate programs of a military type.

I cannot, nor would, carry these observations further; I shall rather confine myself to putting the question that seems important at this point, a question that only the future can answer:

"What will be the result for the value of culture? What will become of independence of mind, independence in the pursuit of knowledge, and above all, independence of feeling? What will become of intellectual freedom?"

146

Let us leave that and come back to France, and consider our own system of education and instruction.

I am obliged to remark that our system, or rather what passes for it (for, after all, I do not know whether we have, or whether what we have can be called, a *system*) . . . I am obliged to remark that our schools share in the general uncertainty and disorder of our time. And, indeed, they so exactly reflect that chaotic state, a state of such remarkable confusion and incoherence, that we have only to look at our programs and objectives of study to understand the mental condition of our time, and discover every aspect of our doubt and our fluctuations with regard to values of every kind. Our school program is not, as in the countries I have mentioned, clearly dominated by a policy. It is mixed with politics, which is quite a different matter; and mixed in an irregular and inconsistent way. We may say that it is free, but as we ourselves are free, with a freedom restrained at one moment for fear of too much, and revived the next for fear of too little. Hardly have we taken courage from a surge of strength when we bristle against any manifestation of it.

Our education, then, shows its uncertainty and does so in its own way. Its aims are divided between tradition and progress. At times, it advances resolutely, sketching out programs that make a clean sweep of many literary or scientific traditions; at other times, a respectable solicitude for what is called the *humanities* lays hold of it, and once again we see the revival of that unending and familiar dispute between the dead and the living, in which the living do not always have the advantage. I cannot fail to observe that in our debates and our vacillation, the fundamental questions are never stated. I know that the problem is terribly difficult. The steady increase in kinds of knowledge is not easily reconciled with the desire to preserve certain qualities which, rightly or wrongly, we consider not only superior in themselves but characteristic of our nation. But if we considered the *subject* of all education —the *child* who is to be made into a man—and if we asked what, precisely, we want that child to become, it seems to me that the problem would be remarkably and happily transformed, and that every program, every method of instruction could be compared point by point with the desired change in the child and the direction that change is to take, and could be judged in that light. Suppose, for example, that we should say:

"This child (taken at random) is to be given the notions he will need in order eventually to add to the nation a man capable of earning his living, of living in the modern world in which he will have to live, of adding a useful ingredient to it, one that will not be dangerous but capable of working toward the general prosperity. Capable, moreover, of enjoying all the different achievements of civilization, and of adding to them; capable, in short, of costing others as little as possible and of bringing them as much as possible. . . ."

I do not say that this formula is definitive or complete, or even at all satisfactory. I say that we must fix our minds upon this order of questions before all else, if we wish to determine the principles of education. It is clear that first of all we must inculcate in young people the fundamental conventions that will enable them to carry on relations with their fellows, and the notions that eventually will give them the means of developing their powers or of guarding against their weaknesses in the social milieu. But when we examine the present state of affairs, we are astonished to see how obviously the methods in use—if methods they are (and if they are not merely a combination of routine, on the one hand, and experimentation or rash anticipation, on the other)—show the lack of prior reflection, which I consider essential. The dominant preoccupation seems to be to give children a culture that is split between the so-called *classical* tradition and the natural desire to initiate them into the vast modern developments in knowledge and activity. Sometimes one tendency is uppermost, sometimes the other; but never, in all the discussion, does the essential question come up:

"*What do we and should we want?*"

The fact is that the question implies a decision, a side to be taken. What we have to do is imagine the *man of our time*, and situate this *idea of man* in the probable surroundings in which he will live. The idea must result from precise observation and not from the feelings and preferences of this person or that—and particularly not from their political hopes. Nothing is more reprehensible, more pernicious, and more misguided than party politics in matters of education. Yet there is one point on which everyone is agreed and deplorably at one. Let us confess: the *real* object of education is the *diploma*.

I never hesitate to declare that the diploma is the deadly enemy of culture. As diplomas have become more important in our lives (and their importance has done nothing but grow as a result of economic conditions), the less has education had any real effect. As regulations have multiplied, the results have grown worse.

Worse in their effect on the public mind and on the mind generally. Worse because a diploma creates hopes and the illusion that certain rights have been acquired. Worse because of the stratagems and subterfuges it gives rise to: the recommendations, the strategic "cramming," and, indeed, the use of every expedient for crossing the redoubtable threshold.

That, we must admit, is a strange and detestable preparation for intellectual and civic life.

Furthermore, if I take my stand on experience alone and look at the effects of regulation in general, I note that regulation will, in all matters, finally vitiate action and pervert it. . . . I have already said so: once an action is put under regulations, the ulterior aim of the one who acts is no longer the action itself. He anticipates the regulations, and thinks how to circumvent them. Examinations are merely a particular case and a striking proof of this very general observation.

With us, the basic diploma is the *baccalauréat*. It has led to adapting the various studies to a strictly defined program with a view to the examinations which, for the examiners, the professors, and the victims, represent, more than anything else, a total, radical, and uncompensated loss of time and labor. The day you create a well-defined regulator like the diploma, you are bound at once to see a whole organization, no less well defined than your program, lining up against it with the sole aim of capturing that diploma by every means. The aim of education being no longer the development of the mind but the acquisition of the diploma, the required minimum becomes the goal of study. It is no longer a matter of learning Latin, Greek, or geometry. It is a matter of *borrowing*—not of *acquiring*—of borrowing what is needed to get the *baccalauréat*.

That is not all. The diploma grants to society a phantom guarantee; and to the diploma-holders, phantom rights. The diploma-holder is officially considered to *know*; all his life he keeps that certificate of some momentary and purely expedient knowledge. Moreover, the holder of a diploma is led in the name of the law to believe that something is owed to him. No practice ever instituted was more fatal for everyone, the State and the individual (and, in particular, for culture). It is with a view to the diploma, for example, that the reading of authors has been replaced by the use of summaries, manuals, absurd digests of knowledge, ready-made collections of questions and answers, extracts, and other abominations. The result is that nothing in this adulterated form of culture can be helpful or suitable to the life of a developing mind.

I do not wish to examine in detail the various subjects taught in our regrettable system of education. I shall confine myself to showing you to what extent the mind is shocked and wounded in its most sensitive part by such a system.

Let us not go into the question of Greek and Latin; the vicissitudes in the history of these studies is a mockery. By ebb and flow, a little Greek, a little Latin, is added to or withdrawn from the program. But what Greek and what Latin! The quarrel about the so-called "humanities" is merely a fight over the semblances of culture. When we see the use to which those unhappy, twice-dead languages are put, we have the impression of some strange fraud. They are no longer dealt with as real languages or literatures; these tongues seem never to have been spoken but by ghosts. For the immense majority of those who make a pretense of studying them, they are bizarre conventions that have no function but to make up the difficult part of an examination. No doubt Latin and Greek have greatly changed within the past century. Antiquity, nowadays, is no longer at all what it was for Rollin, any more than the "Apollo Belvedere" and the "Laocoön" have been considered, for the past hundred years, the masterpieces of ancient sculpture; nor is there any doubt that no one now knows the Latin of the Jesuits or that of the doctors of philology. Some know a sort of Latin, or rather make a pretense of knowing a sort of Latin, whose final and only use is in the translation required for the *baccalauréat*. For my part, I believe it would be better to make the teaching of dead languages entirely optional, with no examination required, and to give only a few students a solid knowledge of them rather than force all of them to swallow indigestible scraps of languages that never existed. . . . I shall believe in the teaching of ancient languages when, in a railway carriage, I see one passenger out of a thousand take a small Thucydides or a charming Virgil from his pocket and become absorbed in it, trampling under foot the newspapers and the more or less *pulp* stories.

But let us go on to French. On this head it will suffice to point out an enormity: France is the one country in the world where it is absolutely impossible to learn to speak French. Go to Tokyo, to Hamburg, to Melbourne, and there it is not unlikely that you will be taught to pronounce your language correctly. But make a tour of France, that is to say, a tour of its accents, and you will discover Babel. Nothing is less surprising: true French is spontaneously spoken only in those regions where French arose. What, on the contrary, may astonish the observer, but seems not to astonish educators, is that the various pronunciations of French—the accents of Marseilles, Picardy, Lyons, Limoges, Corsica, or Alsace—in a country whose keen interest in unification is well known, have not been reformed and corrected so that all Frenchmen may recognize their tongue throughout the land.

Here we encounter the misdeeds of spelling. Let us run over the provinces of our country. We shall find in the various types of local speech that French vowels are generally altered from one province to another. On the other hand, we shall observe that the structure of words, the articulated form that is in some way held in shape by the *consonants*, is rigorously, much too rigorously, sounded by all those mouths in conformity with our criminal spelling. We find, for example, that all consonants which are doubled in writing, and which should not be heard in French, are terribly emphasized in speaking. Everything is pronounced. For example, people say *somptueux* and *dompter* instead of *sontueux* and *donter*. . . . And, in my part of the country, the South, we say: *La valeur n'attend pas le nombre des an-nées.*

This is not the place to bring the whole of our orthography to trial. The absurdity of our spelling, which is indeed one of the most grotesque fabrications in the world, is well known. It is an imperious or imperative collection of a great many errors in etymology, artificially fixed by decisions that are inexplicable. Let us end this trial, but not without observing how the complicated spelling of our language puts it in an inferior position with regard to certain others. Italian is perfectly phonetic, whereas French, in its wealth, has two ways of writing *f*, four ways of writing *k*, two of writing *z*, etc.

I now come back to the spoken language. Do you think that our literature, and in particular our poetry, does not suffer from our negligent training in speech? What do you expect a poet to do, a true poet, a man for whom the *sounds* of a language have an equal importance (equal, I say) to that of the *sense*, when he has carefully formulated his rhythmic structures on the values of voice and tone, and then he hears that special music which is poetry, being read, or rather massacred, in one of the various accents I have mentioned? But even if the accent is that of true French, the way of speaking taught in school is quite simply criminal. Go and hear La

Fontaine or Racine recited in any school you like. Children are instructed literally to drone; and, more than that, not the least notion of rhythm or of the assonances and alliterations that form the sonorous substance of poetry is ever given and demonstrated to them. No doubt these things are considered a waste of time, and yet they are the very substance of poetry. But, contrariwise, candidates for examinations will be required to have a certain knowledge of poetry and poets. What a strange kind of knowledge! Is it not astonishing to substitute a purely abstract knowledge (which in any case has only the remotest connection with poetry) for the sensation itself of hearing the poem? While we are required to respect the absurd part of our language, the spelling, we tolerate the most barbarous misrepresentation of the phonetic part, that is to say, the living language. The basic idea seems to be, here as in other matters, to set up an *easy* means of checking; for nothing is easier than to check the conformity or nonconformity of a written text with the legal spelling, at the expense of real knowledge, which is the experience of poetry. Spelling has become the criterion of good education, while a feeling for the music, for the rhythm and form of phrases, plays no part whatever in classes or examinations. . . .

Education is not confined to childhood and adolescence. Learning is not limited to the schools. Throughout life, our *milieu* is our teacher, at once stern and dangerous. Stern because mistakes here are more costly than in school, and dangerous because we are hardly aware of the educational influence, good or bad, of our milieu and our fellows. We learn something at every moment; but such direct lessons are usually unnoticed. We are made up, to a large extent, of all the events that have affected us, but we are not aware of their effects accumulating and combining within us. Let us look a little more closely at the way in which this chance education transforms us.

I shall distinguish two kinds of accidental learning that go on constantly: one, the good kind, or at least it could be, is *learning from experience*; these are the lessons learned from what happens to us, the facts we directly observe or experience. The more direct the observation—that is to say, the more directly we perceive things or events or people, without immediately translating our impressions into clichés and ready-made expressions—the more valuable are the perceptions. I add (and this is not a paradox) that a direct perception is all the more precious as we are the less able to express it. The more it defies the resources of our language, the more it forces us to develop them.

We have within us a whole reserve of phrases, epithets, and ready locutions which are made by pure imitation; they rid us of the trouble of thinking, because we tend to take them for valid and appropriate solutions.

For the most part, we react to what strikes us by using words that are not ours; we are not their true authors. Our thought—or what we take to be our thought—is, at such times, merely a simple, automatic response. That is why we must not too readily believe *our own words*. I mean that a word that comes into our head is generally not ours.

But where does it come from? Here we see the second type of learning I mentioned. This is the learning that comes, not from our direct personal experience, but from our reading or from what we are told.

You know, though perhaps you have not thought much about it, how *talkative* the modern age is. Our cities are plastered with gigantic letters. The night itself is peopled with words of fire. In the morning, numberless printed sheets are in the hands of passers-by, of travelers in trains, and lazy people in their beds. We have only to turn a knob in our room to hear the voices of the world and sometimes our masters' voice. As for books, never have so many been published. Never has so much been read, or rather, skimmed over!

What will be the result of this great debauch?

The same as I was describing just now; but this time it is our verbal sensibility that is being brutalized, dulled, degraded. Our inner language is wearing out.

Adjectives are devaluated. The inflation of publicity has depleted the power of the strongest epithets. Praise and even abuse are in bad straits; we have to cudgel our brains to find the means of praising or insulting anyone!

Furthermore, the daily output of vast quantities of published matter, the flood of printing and broadcasting, wash over our judgments and impressions from morning to night, mangling and mixing them, making of our brains truly a gray matter in which nothing stands out, nothing can last, and we have an odd sense of the monotony of novelty; we are bored with wonders and extremes.

What must we conclude from such observations?

For all their incompleteness, I think they are enough to give us grave anxieties about the future of intelligence—I mean intelligence as we have known it. We have in our minds a notion of the mind, and various standards of intellectual value which, though very ancient—not to say immemorial— are perhaps not eternal.

For example, we can still hardly imagine that the labor of the mind could be collective. The individual seems indispensable to any advance in the highest forms of knowledge, and to all production in the arts. For myself, I hold fast to this opinion, though I recognize that it is based on personal feeling and that feeling is suspect: the stronger it is, the more personal; and I tell myself that we must not try to read the lines of the future in one person. So I refrain from pronouncing on the great enigmas posed by the modern era. I see that it is putting our minds through unimagined trials.

All the notions by which we have lived are tottering. The sciences are calling the tune. Time, space, and matter are as though in the furnace, and our categories are in fusion.

As for political principles and economic laws, you know well enough that, today, Mephistopheles in person seems to have enrolled them in his hellish crew.

Lastly, we are faced with the difficult and controversial question of the relations between the individual and the State: the State, which is to say, an organization that is growing tighter, more demanding, more efficient every day, taking whatever portion it wants of the individual's freedom, his work, his time, his strength, and, in short, his life, giving him in return . . . What? The means to enjoy what is left, develop what is left? The shares are difficult to determine. It would seem that at present the State has the upper hand, that its power tends to absorb almost the entire individual.

But the individual stands for the mind's freedom. Now we have seen that freedom (in the highest sense) is becoming, under the conditions of modern life, an illusion. We are hypnotized, harassed, stupefied, a victim of all the contradictions, the dissonances that rend the air of modern civilization. The individual is already compromised, even before the State has entirely assimilated him.

I have said that I shall not draw conclusions, but I will end with something in the way of advice.

Among the features of our epoch, there is one I shall speak no ill of. I am no enemy of sports. . . . I mean those sports that do not depend on mere imitation and fashion, on whatever makes a great noise in the newspapers. But it is the *idea* of sports that I like. And I like to transpose it into the realm of the mind. It is an idea that leads us to cultivate one of our native qualities to its highest point while keeping them all in balance; for a sport that deforms its subject is a bad sport. Well, any sport seriously practiced is a test requiring privations (sometimes severe ones), hygiene, concentration, and regularity, all measured by the results—in short, a true morality of action that tends to develop the human type through a training based on the analysis and systematic stimulation of one's abilities. It might be characterized in a phrase, a seeming paradox, by saying that it consists in the training of our reflexes by reflection.

But the mind, though a mind, can deal with itself by similar methods. The functioning of our mind may be considered as a flow of unconscious production irregularly interrupted by consciousness. Mentally we are a succession of transformations, some of which—the conscious ones—are more complex than the other, the unconscious ones. At one moment we dream, at another we wake: that roughly expresses the matter. Well, every positive, unquestionable increase in human potentiality is due to the functioning of these two modes of psychic life, with a resulting increase of consciousness—that is to say, an increase of willed inner action. If civilized man thinks in quite a different way from primitive man, it is due to the predominance in him of conscious reactions over unconscious products. Of course the latter are the indispensable, and sometimes most valuable, substance of our thoughts, but their lasting value depends in the end on consciousness.

Intellectual sport, then, consists in the development and control of our inner acts. Just as the virtuoso of the piano or the violin manages artificially, by studying himself, to increase his consciousness of his own impulses and finally to possess them distinctly, thus attaining a higher order of freedom, so must we, in the order of intellect, acquire an art of thinking, fashion for ourselves a kind of controlled psychology. . . . Such is the blessing I wish for you.

Remarks on Progress

[1929]

ARTISTS used not to like what was called Progress. They found no more of it in works of art than philosophers did in manners. They condemned the barbarous behavior of science, the engineer's brutal operations on the landscape, the tyranny of machines, the simplification of human types as a result of the growing complexity of collective organization. Around 1840 they were already indignant about the effects of a transformation that had hardly begun. Though they were contemporaries of Ampère and Faraday, the Romantics readily ignored the sciences, or despised them, or fastened only on the fantastic in them. Their minds sought refuge in a version of the Middle Ages they had fashioned for themselves; they shunned the chemist for the alchemist. They were happy only with legend or history—that is, with the exact opposite of physics. They escaped from organized life into passion and emotion, and on these they founded a culture (and even a type of drama).

Here, however, is a rather striking contradiction in the intellectual behavior of a great man of that period. The same Edgar Poe who was one of the first to denounce the new barbarism and the cult of the modern, was also the first writer who thought of bringing to the production of literature, to the art of writing fiction, and even to poetry, the very spirit of analysis and calculation whose exploits and transgressions he elsewhere deplored.

In short, the idol of Progress was countered by the idol of damning Progress; which made *two commonplaces*.

As for us, we hardly know what to think of the prodigious changes that are taking place around us and even within us. New powers, new constraints; and the world has never been less sure where it was going.

As I was thinking of the artist's antipathy for progress, a few related ideas came to mind; I offer them for what they are worth—as idle as you please.

In the first half of the nineteenth century the artist discovered and defined his opposite—the *bourgeois*. The bourgeois is the Romantic's other face. Moreover, he is saddled with contradictory qualities, for he is made out to be at one and the same time the slave of routine and an absurd partisan of progress. The bourgeois loves stability, yet believes in improvement. He is the incarnation of common sense and devotion to palpable reality, but he trusts in a kind of increasing and almost inevitable betterment of living standards. The artist claims the world of "dreams."

Now the passage of time—or, if you like, the demon of unexpected combinations (a demon who derives the most surprising consequences from the present, and out of these composes the future)—amused itself by making a quite admirable muddle out of two exactly opposite notions. What happened was that the miraculous and the scientific contracted an astonishing alliance; these two old enemies conspired to involve our lives in an endless career of transformations and surprises. Men are doubtless developing the habit of considering all knowledge as transitional, and every stage of their industry and their relations as provisional. This is new. The rules of collective life must more and more take account of the unexpected. The real is no longer neatly delimited. Place, time, and matter admit of liberties that, not long ago, no one had an inkling of. Logic begets dreams. Dreams take on flesh. Common sense, a hundred times confounded, baffled by the success of the most extraordinary experiments, is now appealed to only by the ignorant. The value of ordinary evidence has gone down to zero. The fact of being commonly accepted, which once made judgments and opinions invincible, today depreciates them. *What was once believed by all, always and everywhere, seems no longer to carry much weight.* The kind of certainty that used to emanate from the unanimity of minds or from the testimony of a large number of people is now contested by the objectivity of records, kept and interpreted by a small number of specialists. Perhaps the value that used to be attached to general consent (on which our manners and civil laws are based) resulted merely from the pleasure the majority always feel at finding themselves in accord and so much like their fellows.

In short, nearly all the dreams of humanity, as found in fables of various types—flying, deep-sea diving, apparitions, speech caught and transmitted, detached from its time and source, and many strange things that no one ever dreamed of —have now emerged from the impossible, from the mind. The fabulous is an article of trade. The manufacture of machines to work miracles provides a living for thousands of people. But the artist has had no share in producing these wonders. They are the work of science and capital. The bourgeois has invested his money in phantoms and is speculating on the downfall of common sense.

Louis XIV, at the height of his power, hadn't the hundredth part of the authority over Nature, the means of amusement, of cultivating his mind, or of providing it with sensations, which are today at the disposal of so many men of moderate station. True, I am not taking into account the pleasure of commanding, subjugating, intimidating, dazzling, punishing, or absolving, which is a godlike and theatrical pleasure. But rather the time, the distance, the speed, the freedom, the view of the whole earth. . . .

A young man today, healthy and in easy circumstances, can fly where he will, quickly circling the earth, sleeping every night in a palace. He can share a hundred ways of life, a taste of love, a taste of security, almost anywhere. If he is not without intelligence (but no more intelligent than need be), he can pick and choose the best of everything, making himself time and again a happy man. The greatest monarch is less to be envied. The body of the great Louis was much less at ease than his, whether a matter of cold or heat, skin or muscles. For when the king was ill, he was poorly doctored. He had to writhe and groan on his feather bed amid all his pomp, with no hope of the quick relief or the unconsciousness that chemistry brings to the least afflicted of moderns.

So, for ills and boredom, and for the satisfaction of curiosities of all kinds, a great many men are now better off than the most powerful man in Europe two hundred and fifty years ago.

Suppose that the enormous transformation which we are living through and which is changing us, continues to develop, finally altering whatever customs are left and making a very different adaptation of our needs to our means; the new era will soon produce men who are no longer attached to the past by any habit of mind. For them history will be nothing but strange, almost incomprehensible tales; there will be nothing in their time that was ever seen before—nothing from the past will survive into their present. Everything in man that is not purely physiological will be altered, for our ambitions, our politics, our wars, our manners, our arts are now in a phase of quick change; they depend more and more on the positive sciences and hence less and less on what used to be. *New facts* tend to take on the importance that once belonged to tradition and *historical facts*.

Even now, a native of some new country, visiting Versailles, may and should look upon those personages laden with their vast wigs, dressed in embroidery, and nobly fixed in stately attitudes, with the same eye as when, at the Ethnographical Museum, we look at the figures clothed in feathers or hides, representing the priests and chiefs of extinct tribes.

One of the surest and cruelest effects of progress, then, is to add a further pain to death, a pain increasing of itself as the revolution in customs and ideas becomes more marked and rapid. It is not enough to perish; one has to become unintelligible, almost ridiculous; and even a Racine or a Bossuet must take his place alongside those bizarre figures, striped and tattooed, exposed to passing smiles, and somewhat frightening, standing in rows in the galleries and gradually blending with the stuffed specimens of the animal kingdom. . . .

I tried years ago to form a positive idea of what is called *progress*. Eliminating all considerations of a moral, political, or aesthetic character, I found that progress came down to the rapid and obvious growth of the (mechanical) *power* at man's disposal, and of the *accuracy* he can attain in his predictions. Horsepower and the number of verifiable decimals: these are indexes that, beyond any doubt, have greatly risen in the last hundred years. Think of what is consumed every day by all the motors of every kind, think of the squandering of resources going on in the world. A Paris street teems and quivers like a factory. In the evening, an orgy of lights, whole treasuries of brilliance pour out before our half-dazzled eyes their extraordinary power of dissipation, their almost criminal largesse. Perhaps waste itself has become a public and permanent necessity. Who knows what might be revealed by a prolonged analysis of such excesses, now becoming so familiar? Perhaps some fairly remote observer, considering the state of our civilization, might conclude that the Great War was but a terrible yet direct and inevitable consequence of the development of our capacities. The scope, duration, intensity, even the atrocity of that war were on the same grand scale as our power. The war itself was of the same magnitude as our peacetime resources and industries; as different in its proportions from previous wars as our weapons, our material resources, and our superabundance *required*. But the difference was not only one of proportion. In the world of physics a thing cannot be made larger without being partially transformed in its *quality*; it is only in pure geometry that figures can be similar. Similitude is almost nowhere but in the heart's desire. The last war cannot be considered a mere enlargement on former conflicts. Wars of the past used to end long before the nations engaged in them were really exhausted—just as, for a single "man" lost, a good chess player will give up the game. It was therefore by a sort of *convention* that the "show" used to end, and the event that revealed the inequality of forces was more symbolic than actual. We, on the other hand, only a few years back, saw a quite modern war continue inevitably to the final exhaustion of the adversaries, all of whose resources, even to the farthest, were brought one after the other to be consumed on the line of fire. Joseph de Maistre's celebrated saying that a battle is lost because it is thought to be lost has itself lost some of its ancient truth. Henceforth the battle is *really* lost because of the shortage of men, gold, bread, coal, and oil, not only in the armies but in the whole country.

Among the many advances made, none is more astonishing than the progress of light. A few years ago, light was an event only for the eyes. There was either light or no light. It spread through space, encountering matter, which more or less modified it but remained foreign to it. Now it has become the world's prime enigma. Its speed expresses and limits something essential to the universe. It is thought to have weight. The study of its radiation is destroying our previous ideas of empty space and pure time. It resembles and is yet different from matter, in a mysterious mixture of ways. Finally, this same light that once was the common symbol of full, distinct, and perfect knowledge, is now involved in a sort of intellectual scandal. It is compromised, together with its accomplice, matter, in the suit brought by discontinuity against continuity, probability against images, integers against complex numbers, analysis against synthesis, hidden reality against the mind that would track it down—and, in a word, by the unintelligible against the intelligible. Science seems to be facing its crucial trial. But the case will be settled out of court.

Our Destiny and Literature

[1937]

THE MIND has transformed the world, and the world is re-paying it in kind. The mind has led man where he had no notion of going. It has given us a taste for life and the means of living, it has conferred on us a power of action enormously surpassing the individual's powers of adaptation and even his capacity for understanding; it has aroused desires and pro-duced results from them greatly exceeding what is useful to life. Hence we have moved farther and farther away from the primitive conditions of all life, borne along as we are at a speed now growing so great as to be terrifying, toward a state of things whose complexity, instability, and inherent disorder bewilder us, allowing us not the least foresight, taking away our ability to reason about the future or to make out any of the lessons we used to expect of the past, and dissolving in their violence and fluctuation all effort at founding and build-ing, whether intellectually or socially, just as quicksands absorb the strength of an animal that ventures upon them.

All this necessarily reacts on the mind itself. A world transformed by the mind no longer presents to the mind the same perspectives and directions as before; it poses entirely new problems and countless enigmas.

The spectacle of the world of man, as man used to see it and as history represented it, partook of both comedy and

167

tragedy; it was easy, comparing one century to another, to find analogous situations, comparable public figures, well-divided periods, long-pursued policies, clearly defined events with fully realized consequences. In those days administrations could live on "precedents."

But how strangely is this classic spectacle transformed! To the human comedy and tragedy has been added an element of the fairy-play. On the stage of the modern world, as on that of the Châtelet Theater, every scene is a transformation scene: nothing but apparitions, quick changes, and surprises, not always pleasant ones. And sometimes the very author of all this, man—at least the man who still has leisure for the lamentable habit of reflection—is astonished at being able to live in the present atmosphere of enchantment and transformation, where contradictions come true, where reverses and catastrophes dispute the stage, one replacing the other as by magic; where, in a mere few years, some invention in the laboratory can be developed and exploited to the point of changing our manners and our minds. And the man who thinks (or can still think) sometimes feels an extraordinary sort of weariness. He feels that the most surprising discovery could no longer surprise him.

I have a granddaughter who is two years and two months old. She uses the telephone nearly every day, she turns the knobs of the radio set, somewhat at random, and, for her, all this is just as natural as playing with her blocks and dolls. I would not for anything lag behind my grandchild, so I am doing my best to give up seeing any distinction between what used to be called natural and what used to be called artificial. . . .

Just now I uttered the term "fairy-play." I was thinking of an old play of this type which I cannot remember whether I read or saw many years ago. A wicked magician was inflicting strange tribulations on an unhappy youth whose love affairs he wished to thwart. At one moment he would surround him with flames and devils, at the next he would change his bed into a pitching and rolling ship in a room inundated by a make-believe sea, and the sheet would swell like a homemade spanker-sail filled with an off-stage wind. . . . But the young man's astonishment finally turned into resigned indifference, and at the wonder-working magician's tenth trick, being bored with all the hocus-pocus, all those tiresome miracles, he shrugged his shoulders and cried:

"Here we go again with that stupid nonsense!"

This, perhaps, is how we shall one day greet the "miracles of science."

But mankind seems never to get enough of them. Besides, I am not sure whether man is aware that he is himself changing. He still believes that "human nature never changes." We *believe* it! . . . which is to say that we know nothing about it! And yet there are reasons for believing that man *is* changing. Just imagine (since we are in the realm of magic) . . . imagine the remarks that might be made by an observer, some Mephistopheles standing a little above mankind, a spectator of the destinies of our race, meditating on our condition, the life of our species as a whole, what is happening, how our life is being transformed, how it has been spent for the past century. He would have plenty of opportunity for amusement at our expense as he noted how curiously our efforts at invention turn against us. While we imagine that we are subjecting forces and matter to our own ends, there is not one of our scientific raids on Nature that does not, on the contrary, directly or indirectly subject us a little more to herself, making us slaves of our own power, creatures all the more incomplete as we are better equipped, making our desires, needs, and very existence the playthings of our own genius.

"Can you not see," that clear-eyed devil would say, "that you are merely the subjects of an outrageous experiment— that thousands of reactions and thousands of unknown substances are being tried out on you? Someone wants to know how your organs will react at very high speeds and very low pressures; whether your blood can adapt itself to highly carburized air; whether your retina can stand stronger and stronger light and radiation. . . . Not to mention the smells and noises you endure, the vibrations and currents of all frequencies, the synthetic foods and goodness knows what else! . . . And as for your intellects, my friends, and your sensibilities—since these are what I am most interested in— your mind is being subjected to an incredible amount of incoherent news every twenty-four hours; your senses have to absorb, without a day's respite, as much music, painting, drugs, and bizarre drinks . . . spectacles, journeys, sudden changes in altitude, in temperature, or in political and economic anxiety as, once upon a time, the whole of humanity was able to absorb in three centuries!

"You are guinea pigs, my dear men, and very ill-used guinea pigs, since the ordeals inflicted on you are repeated and varied merely at random. There is no scientist, no laboratory assistant to regulate, measure, check, and interpret the experiments, the artificial changes whose more or less profound effect on your precious persons no one can foresee. Fashion and industry, the combined forces of invention and advertising possess you, lay you out on the beaches, send you up to the snows, tan your thighs, and bleach your hair; while politics lines up your multitudes, makes them raise their hands or brandish their fists, march in step, vote, hate or love or die in cadence, indistinguishably, like mere statistics!"

But I must silence my Mephistopheles. He was about to give the whole show away! But, devil though he is, he would certainly not have been able to tell you the future. The future is like everything else, no longer what it used to be. By that I mean that we cannot now think of it with any degree of confidence in our inductions. We have lost our traditional means of thinking about and predicting it: this is the pathos of our plight.

Though we are more and more anxious to know where we are going and never tired of wondering about the possibilities of the morrow, yet we live a terribly everyday life. We live from day to day—as people lived in those ages that were most harried by immediate needs, the most precarious periods of humanity. But still, and as though to deepen our sense of uncertainty, we are not yet accustomed to doing without predictions, we are not yet prepared to live simply in the present, in spurts and snatches. Our deeply ingrained habits, our laws, our language, our feelings, our ambitions were formed at a time and attuned to a time that allowed long duration, basing itself and its reasoning on an immense past, and having in view a future measured by generations.

Moreover, the same is true of our relation to space. Our customs, ambitions, politics are all inspired by notions that are strongly, powerfully local; they are suited to men bound to the soil, settled. Whether in reference to individuals or nations, our ideas, laws, conflicts, and contracts imply stability, recognition of property rights, and control of territory. In short, duration and continuity of nations and individuals

... these are still at the basis of our institutions. Think of marriage, inheritance, our idea of ourselves; we think we are individuals!... But location and permanence, once the foundations of our social and political life, are now more and more in contradiction with the impulse to movement which torments the modern world, and with all the facilities we have created to satisfy our longing for escape and our odd ideal of ubiquity.

And so, in conflict with rooted man, we have mobile man. We are witnessing a desperate struggle between our ancient framework and our growing power of movement. While our new type of nomad sits astride five or six hundred horsepower, and flies over territorial boundaries, ignoring frontiers and Customs, our modern nations are setting up between themselves higher and higher barriers—which they would gladly raise to the heavens. Indeed, they are striving more and more to do without each other, which leads them into curiously contradictory behavior; for while each nation tends to become an autonomous system, a closed economy, an autarky (as the saying is today), they are doing their best to produce far more than they can consume, with the naïve idea of selling this surplus abroad while taking as little as possible of the surplus of others.

This reaction against complete mobility, however, is not without a few advantages. If humanity should proceed without hindrance toward the highest speeds, toward constant motion and almost instantaneous communication, we should have to stop regulating our watches by the sun; that star would be eliminated from timing our actions, day could no longer be distinguished from night, and we should have to adopt sidereal time, that of the fixed stars (which, incidentally, are not fixed, since nothing is).

After dinner, in one and the same instant of time or perception, you can be in New York by ear (soon it will be by eye) while your cigarette sends up its smoke in Paris. This is in the true sense of the word a dislocation, which will not be without its consequences. In short, if we bring together and try to set in order all the observations we can make regarding the changes in the world today, we find ourselves at grips with a paradoxical idea trying to take shape in our minds, where it clashes with ancient knowledge and immemorial habits.

We are unable (up to now, absolutely unable) to admit that a kind of ignorance, a helplessness of the mind, can equal a positive knowledge. We are unable to consider as a real gain the well-established conviction that a conscious refusal to exercise our intellect may be an act of intelligence, and still less are we able to regard as characteristic of a thing, and as one of the essential points of its definition, the fact that that thing is indeterminate. You would think it ridiculous if someone should answer you, on being asked his name:

"My name? Whatever you like!"

You would find the answer absurd. And if he should add: "My name is whatever you like, and that is actually my name," you would think him mad. And yet, that is perhaps what we shall have to get accustomed to: indeterminateness as a positive fact, a positive element of knowledge.

. . . .

People used to say, quite commonly (it is proverbial): "You never know what's coming." But no one saw the true profundity of this banal remark. The man who first uttered it, and those who repeated it after him, doubtless meant simply to express the experience of their past lives. They had observed that something unexpected was constantly happening and that the slightest glance at anyone's history shows a sequence of unforeseen events, and predictions proved wrong. But I find a more interesting meaning in the rather trite wisdom of this old proposition. I interpret it this way: the living organs, their functions, and those of the mind, all the properties and faculties of the living man are what enables us to adapt, in some degree, to what will happen. My eye is unaware that I am nearing a certain object, or that the light will change in intensity; and yet, as soon as the object comes nearer, as soon as the light gets stronger or weaker, my eye is at once modified in order to preserve its clear vision. Therefore it was capable of being modified—which could be translated into rather unphilosophic language by saying that it was made to be modified, that it was made for this unexpected event, that it foresaw something unforeseen, that certain previous incidents had perhaps shaped and adapted it to this end, and that its ability to accommodate was as though made for surprises, and that the eye is not only an organ of sight but an instrument endowed with foresight. . . .

If, now, you generalize from this simple example . . . if you observe that the whole man (and not only the whole man, but the whole complex web of his life) hangs, as it were, on the possibility of being modified in face of an event, so that the man and his complexity may preserve what is required to keep on living, for the self to maintain its continuity, recognize itself and go on being itself, you will easily understand how essential is the role of a certain "free play" in the very structure of our organism, our mind, and our society. All three admit of a certain free play, a capacity for adapting to a certain amount of the unexpected. Besides, such ideas as forethought, precaution, prudence, our civil laws, marriage,

174

credit, debt, and the investment of money all presuppose that the morrow—unknowable though it may be in detail—cannot be entirely different from today. In a word, it used to be that all the events of life which the mind might be uncertain about were somehow set out before it; they were imaginable, they belonged to recognized species which man had known and described from remotest antiquity. There were limits to the unforeseen, and this conferred great value on history, which taught us that one might, by and large, expect what had already been. Of course our fathers used to say that chance played a great part; they knew that no one could be sure of the outcome of any affair; but on the whole, this imaginable kind of contingency allowed them to decree lasting laws, to sign stable agreements, to lay up savings for their children, to know, when buying, exactly what they would have to pay and, when selling, what they would receive. Do we still know?

. . . .

I was saying that the unexpected itself has been in process of transformation and that today its scope is almost boundless. Imagination faints before it. It used to be that in foresight our vision (and, consequently, the unforeseen at that time) was limited on the one hand by our knowledge and on the other by our means of action, and these two factors were somehow in balance. We regarded the unknown future simply as a combination of things already known; the new could be broken down into elements that were not new. But this is no longer so. Here is an image of things as they now are, or so it seems to me:

Instead of playing a straightforward card game with destiny, as we used to do, knowing the rules, knowing the number of cards and face cards, we are now in the position of a player who discovers with amazement that his partner's hand contains face cards he has never seen before, and that the rules of the game change with every deal. No calculation of probability is possible and he cannot even throw the cards in his opponent's face. Why? Because the more he looks at him the more he recognizes himself!... The modern world is being remade in the image of man's mind. Man has sought in Nature the means and power to make things around him as restless, as unstable, as mobile as himself... as admirable, absurd, disconcerting, and wonderful as his own mind. Now the mind is unpredictable, nor can it predict itself. We can predict neither our dreams nor our plans; we can predict little but our reactions. If then we impose on the human world the ways of the mind, the world becomes just as unpredictable; it takes on the mind's disorder.

However, we must consider as best we can (and naturally without any pretension to prophecy) the question of the future—the destiny, if you like—of literature. It already bears certain mysterious signs on its forehead.

Literature may be affected first of all in the person of the one who practices it; and next, in the matter it is made of, language, and in the ways in which language changes. Finally, apart from the author and the work, literature necessarily involves a third condition, which can itself vary, and which is none other than the reader.

Considered in the person of the author, literature is a curious profession. Its tools are merely a pen and a few sheets of paper; the apprenticeship, the learning of the craft, is whatever you please: it may last for a moment or forever. The raw material is also whatever you wish. It is everywhere—in the street, in the heart, in good and evil. And as for the labor involved, it is indefinable; anyone can say that he belongs to this profession and means to master it.

But let us now consider with an unindulgent eye the writer's odd social situation. Strip him of the luster he still traditionally wears and look at him in his real life as an artisan of ideas, a practitioner of written language. What or whom does he remind us of, busy beneath his lamp, shut in by his books and his walls, strangely absorbed or agitated, in the grip of some curious discussion, the subject of which is invisible; now animated, then suddenly stopping short, but finally and always coming back to his work table and scribbling, or rattling his typewriter? Set aside the romantic image of the disheveled poet, with fateful brow, feeling as though he were a harp or a lyre in the midst of a tempest, or at night under the moon, beside a lake. . . . Nothing good is ever done in such extraordinary circumstances. Beautiful verse matures on the day after the inspiration.

Now look at the author of a work. What are this worker's circumstances?

In truth, literature, as it really is, is curiously akin to one of those little homecrafts, of which so many are still to be found in Paris; and in many ways it *is* one. The poet reminds us of those ingenious craftsmen who, for Christmas or the New Year, make those toys so remarkable for inventiveness and calculated surprises, out of whatever comes to hand. The poet gets his materials from ordinary language. Though he may invoke heaven and earth, raise up tempests, stir our emotions, or elicit what is most delightful or tragic in the depths of our being, though he may have at his disposal all Nature, death, the infinite, the gods and all beauty, he is nonetheless, in the eyes of anyone observing his deeds and gestures, a citizen, a taxpayer, who shuts himself up at a certain hour in front of a blank notebook and covers it with black scribbles, sometimes in silence, sometimes shouting and pacing back and forth between door and window. About 1840 Victor Hugo was a model author, living like any bourgeois in a flat in the Marais district. He paid his rent and his taxes; he was a regular producer. But what did he do? What did he produce? And what type of industry was it? The same observer, drily accurate, would note that the products of that little industry had a fluctuating value, as precarious as that of a toymaker's products or those of any fancy-goods maker working in his room, a few steps away, in the Rue des Archives or the Rue Vieille-du-Temple.

But that value, the value produced by the poet's hands, is complex, ambivalent, and, in both cases, essentially unstable. It is composed of one part reality (that is, it can sometimes be exchanged for money) and one part smoke— a strange smoke indeed, that may one day solidify into some monumental work of bronze or marble, casting round about it a powerful and enduring aura of fame. But again, whether real or ideal, that value is incommensurable; it cannot be measured in society's terms. A work of art is worth a diamond to some, a pebble to others. It cannot be assessed in man-hours; it cannot, therefore, figure as a universally negotiable currency for every kind of exchange. The useful is that which satisfies men's physiological needs, whose possession frees man from some sensation of pain or deficiency, some physically defined depreciation.

Man acts to appease any such sensation; and the development, organization, and co-ordination of his action, radiating outward to thousands of other beings over the surface of the globe, has given rise to the whole economic machinery. But there is no place in it for the useless. Basically the economic machine is an enlargement, a colossal amplification of the human organism; and such an apparatus, founded strictly on the equal usefulness of all objects and services exchanged by men, cannot accommodate objects and services that satisfy only desires, not absolute needs, and cater only to individual dispositions, not to vital functions. For these reasons any society that is systematically and completely organized cannot, without altering its rigid economy, permit any luxury, any exchange of things having *value for all*, in return for things having *value for some but not for others*.

How, then, have our poets, philosophers, and artists, all our small craftsmen who produce things that are the pride of the human race . . . how have they managed to live, hitherto? They have lived . . . as best they could. Thanks to a loose connection in the economic machine, they have lived—some very badly, some fairly well: Verlaine from hand to mouth and on charity; whereas Victor Hugo left millions. . . . Among my little attic craftsmen, some make a fortune, others a failure; most of them get by with odd jobs on the side: they have to have several strings to their lyre.

But, lucky or not, the general run of human affairs promises them nothing brilliant. Everywhere they are threatened by the rigidity of planned economy. The machine is beginning to function much too mechanically for them; and more than that, the heavy hand of authority, though it occasionally refrains from crushing some thought in embryo, allows only those works to hatch out which sing or proclaim or show that everything is better and better under the best of all possible regimes.

A further consideration: literature, in essence no more than an exploitation of the resources of language, depends on the various changing conditions a language may undergo, and on the modes of transmission provided by the material means at the disposal of the age.

I have no time to develop the many observations that this aspect of the subject calls for. I shall confine myself to a few remarks on radio broadcasting on the one hand and disc recording on the other.

We may already wonder whether a purely spoken and heard literature will not very shortly replace written literature. This would be a return to primitive times, and the technical consequences would be enormous. If writing were dispensed with, what would be the result? First—and this would be to the good—the part played by the voice and the demands of the ear would, in matters of form, resume the capital importance they once had, and still had a few centuries ago. The structure of literary works, their dimensions, would at once be strongly affected; but on the other hand, it would be much more difficult to go back over an author's text. Certain poets would not be able to make themselves as complicated as they are said to be, and readers, transformed into listeners, could no longer look back over a passage, reread it, go into it more deeply, for pleasure, or to criticize it, as they can do with a text held in their hands.

Another thing. Suppose long-distance vision develops (and I must confess that I scarcely hope it will), then the descriptive passages in books could at once be replaced by visual representation: landscapes and portraits would no longer fall within the province of Letters, they would have done with the medium of language. One may go still further. The sentimental passages could likewise be reduced, if not entirely done away with, by introducing amorous pictures and well-chosen music at the tender moments. . . .

And here at last is a possible and perhaps the most serious consequence of setting all this progress in motion. What would become of abstract literature? As long as it is merely a question of amusing, moving, or delighting the mind, we may in a pinch agree that broadcasting is sufficient. But science and philosophy require a quite different rhythm of thought, which reading used to make possible. Or, rather, they require an absence of rhythm. Reflection frequently halts or breaks the movement, introduces unequal pauses, backward glances, and detours, which require the presence of the text and the possibility of handling it at leisure. All this is impossible in listening.

The ear alone is not adequate for the transmission of abstract works.

But I will not dwell on all these very interesting problems, the nature and scope of which we can already see; I shall limit myself, in concluding this point (though not yet in closing), to pushing on toward certain particular points on the literary horizon.

Fantasy is one of the provinces of literature, and I have sometimes asked myself in what new developments it might, today or tomorrow, be put to use. Let me be more specific. What would or could such a maker of imaginary worlds as Jules Verne or H. G. Wells do today? Note that although they invented imaginary worlds, neither of them attempted anything on the intellectual side. For example, they made no effort to imagine the arts of the future. The celebrated Captain Nemo, as everyone knows, plays the organ in his *Nautilus* at the bottom of the ocean, and what he plays is the music of

Bach or Handel. Jules Verne did not foresee our electronic music, nor did he think up new combinations or compositions, nor some yet unknown kind of aesthetics. Remember that it was easy for him to imagine certain inventions that have been made since his time: the submarine, the airplane, etc. These required no more than the elaboration of already existing resources, combined with the naïve fantasies of primitive man, fantasies he has had from the beginning—for instance, flying through the air, traveling undersea, striking someone down at a distance, creating riches without the corresponding toil. All this required no more imagination than what may be termed elementary. Even Wells, in his famous book *The Time Machine*, used and explored time as it used to be, old-fashioned time, the kind of time that had been real down to his day.

But anyone today who wanted to be the successor of these famous storytellers would have to borrow from recent science its paradoxical views and strange predictions. True, he would disconcert his reader and doubtless require of him some rather abstruse knowledge. After all, it would not be impossible to bring into modern literature a truly modern version of the fantastic: for example, having prepared the way with a semblance of scientific explanation, one could introduce a character who, with a gesture or a mere glance at an instrument, produces tremendous effects at a distance—very much like magic. Such magic already exists! We can open a safe by merely speaking a phrase, an "Open, Sesame!" More than that, and with no trick, we know very well (sometimes too well) that a gesture or a glance directed at a human being can often bring about astonishing consequences. For the future, it will be enough to substitute imaginary mechanisms for living persons, making them sensitive to a glance—

an invention requiring little of the writer—and we shall have yet unexploited means of combining the elements of fiction.

But all this is merely derived, roughly, from our present possibilities in physics. We must go a bit further. To think of the destiny of literature is also, and above all, to think of the future of the mind. On this point, everyone is perplexed. Since we are entirely free to conceive the mind's future as we wish, we may arbitrarily suppose either that things will continue to be very like what we know, or that in the coming age there will be a decline in intellectual values, a deterioration and decadence comparable to what happened at the close of antiquity, when culture was abandoned, when works of literature and art were either no longer comprehensible or were destroyed, and the production of such works forbidden. All these things are unhappily quite possible, and possible in two well-known ways: either the tremendous power of our instruments of destruction may be brought into play, decimating the populations of the most cultivated regions of the globe, wrecking the monuments, libraries, laboratories, archives, reducing the survivors to a poverty that would overwhelm their intelligence and suppress all that elevates the mind of man; or else, not the means of destruction, but the very means of possession and enjoyment, with all the incoherence resulting from too frequent and too facile sense impressions, with the rapid and widespread application of industrial methods to the production, evaluation, and consumption of the fruits of the mind, may in the end corrupt the highest and most important intellectual virtues—the powers of attention, meditation, and critical analysis, and what may be called thought in the grand style, or prolonged and profound research carried through to the most precise and forceful expression of its object.

· ·

Let me take a more reassuring view for a moment. I warn you that I am here dealing with the *intellectually fantastic*, with possibilities which, as I told you just now, neither Verne, nor Wells, nor Poe himself, the greatest and most profound author in this genre, dared to imagine. Let us first recall that we know nothing about the mind itself and almost nothing about the senses. I have sometimes remarked to physicists, when the conversation had turned to the many unforeseen innovations that bewilder science today, that, after all, the retina must have its own ideas about light, about the wave phenomena that confound the terms we have taken from traditional language—matter, energy, continuity and discontinuity. . . .

"It is to be predicted," I would say to them, "that, one day or another, you will be forced to concentrate your research on the sensibility and its organs. These are your basic mechanisms. Every measurement you physicists make brings into play: touch, sight, and the muscular sense. With the help of your numerous relays and other instruments, you have gone far beyond the little radius within which all these senses have a hold on something. You began by using the images they perceive, to imagine what you thought existed below the level of the senses; but now you have reached the limit, beyond which those images and analogies are useless. You must come back to the source, back to our little-known senses, which bring us what we know."

We know still less, perhaps, about memory and the other faculties, or properties, of what we call the mind. And yet (and perhaps without knowing more) it is not absurd to

184

imagine that in the not too distant future all our ideas about the mind and its faculties may be shaken up, transformed, as our ideas about the physical world are at present, compared with what they were forty years ago. What we still call intelligence, memory, imagination, genius, talent, etc. are notions and categories that will perhaps seem as crude, primitive, and outdated as the idea of "matter" opposed to "mind" does today. You know, of course, that in the last few years matter has vanished, and with it many a dispute. Spiritualism and materialism now have only historical significance—that of a rather outworn antithesis.

What can happen, then, in this field?

A great scientist of my acquaintance, who still has full confidence in the somewhat shaken theory of evolution, firmly believes that man will finally acquire what he now lacks to resolve the contradictions that today impede him in many fields; that we shall eventually become familiar (in the course of a few hundred centuries) with an entirely new world, characterized by the pre-existence and actual occurrence of vastly different magnitudes, widely separated dimensions and speeds; and that the most abstract notions, those which today are only mathematical symbols without images, will become intuitive in the minds of men in those times.

I confess I am less certain than he that the resources of our nature will bestow such favors on our intelligence, but you have every right to dream of them, and I should not like to detain you any longer from yourselves and your hopes.

Freedom of the Mind

[1939]

IT IS a sign of the times, and not a very good sign, that today it is not only necessary but imperative to interest people's minds in the fate of the Mind—that is, in their own fate.

This necessity is obvious at any rate to men of a certain age (which means, unfortunately, an age that is only too certain) . . . men who have known quite another time, lived quite another life, accepted, suffered, and observed the good and evil things of life in quite other surroundings, in a very different world.

They have admired things that are hardly ever admired now, have seen truths living that are now nearly dead, have in fact speculated on values whose decline or collapse is as clear, as manifest, and as ruinous to their hopes and beliefs as the decline or collapse of the securities and currencies which they, and everyone else, once thought were unshakable values.

They have witnessed the ruin of their former faith in the mind, a faith that was the foundation and, in a way, the postulate of their life.

They had faith in the mind, but what mind? . . . what did they mean by this word? . . .

The word is indecipherable, since it refers to the source and value of all other words. But the men I am thinking of gave it a special meaning. Perhaps they meant by mind that personal yet universal activity, internal and external, which confers on life, on the raw energies of life, on the world, and the reactions provoked in us by the world, a direction and use, a concentration and cumulative effort, or effect, all quite different from those having to do with the normal functioning of ordinary life, the mere preservation of the person.

To comprehend this point correctly we must understand by the word *mind* the ability, the need, and the energy to separate and to develop thoughts and acts which are not necessary to the functioning of our organism, or do not improve its economy.

For the living creature in us, like all living creatures, has to have a certain power, *a power of transformation* that can exert itself on all the things around us, to make us aware of them.

This power of transformation is spent in solving the vital problems imposed on us by our organism and our surroundings.

We are, above all, a system of transformation, more or less complex (according to the species of animal). Since everything that lives must both expend and receive life, the living creature and his surroundings mutually modify each other.

However, once the vital needs are satisfied, there is one species, our own, an *actively* strange species, which thinks it must create other needs and other tasks for itself than that of preserving life. It is concerned with other exchanges, and tempted to other transformations.

Whatever may be the origin, the cause of its curious divergence, the human species has set out on an enormous adventure ... whose aim and end it does not know, and whose limits it imagines it can ignore.

Man has set out on an adventure, and what I call *the mind* has furnished him with the immediate direction, the spur, the stimulus, the impetus, the drive, just as it furnished the pretexts and all the illusions required for action. These pretexts and illusions, by the way, have varied from age to age. The perspective of the intellectual adventure is a shifting one. . . .

This, more or less, is what I meant by my opening remarks.

I want to dwell on this point for a moment so as to show more precisely how our *human* power differs (though not entirely) from our *animal* power—the latter being spent in preserving our life, specializing in the performance of the habitual cycle of our physiological functions.

Our human power is different, but resembles the other and is very closely connected with it. The similarity between them is an important fact and, on reflection, teems with consequences. It may be quite easily shown: we must not forget that whatever we do, whatever the object of our action, whatever the order of impressions we receive from the world around us and whatever our reactions to them, one and the same organism is entrusted with the whole business, the same apparatus of relations is used for the two activities I have indicated: the useful and the useless, the indispensable and the arbitrary.

The same senses, the same muscles, the same limbs; more than that, the same types of signs, the same tokens of exchange, the same languages, the same modes of logic that function in the most indispensable actions of our life, all likewise figure in our most gratuitous, conventional, and extravagant actions.

In short, man does not have two sets of equipment, he has only one; and sometimes it functions to maintain his life, his physiological rhythm, and sometimes it furnishes the illusions and labors of our *great adventure*.

On one subject in particular I have often made a comparison between our two forms of action, saying that the same organs, muscles, nerves, produce both walking and dancing, exactly as our faculty of language serves, on one hand, to express our needs and ideas, while on the other, the same words and forms can combine to produce poetry. In both cases a single mechanism is used for two completely different ends.

It is therefore natural, in speaking of both practical and spiritual matters (meaning by *spiritual* all science, art, philosophy, etc.), that we should note a remarkable parallel between them, and be able sometimes to draw a lesson from it.

Certain rather difficult questions can thus be simplified, by showing the similarity—based on our organs of action and relation—between the activities that may be called *superior* and those that may be called practical or *pragmatic*.

Between the two, since the same organs are involved, there is an analogy of functions, a correspondence of dynamic phases and conditions. All this has a profound substantive origin, since the organism itself governs it.

I was saying just now how sadly affected men of my years are by the times so rapidly and crudely replacing those they once knew; and in this connection I mentioned the word *value*.

I spoke, I believe, of the decline and collapse, before our very eyes, of the values of our life; and with the word *value* I brought together under one term, one sign, values of the material and the spiritual order.

Value is precisely what I wish to talk about, the important point to which I should like to draw your attention.

We are today witnessing a true and gigantic transmutation of values (to use Nietzsche's excellent phrase), and in giving to this lecture the title "Freedom of the Mind" I am simply alluding to one of those essential values which nowadays seem to be suffering the same fate as material values.

So, in saying *value*, I mean that *mind* is a value, just as *oil*, *wheat*, and *gold* are values.

I said *value* because an appraisal, an assessment of importance is involved, and also because there is a price to be discussed—the price we are willing to pay for the value we call *the mind*.

We may have made an investment in this value; we can "follow" it, as they say on the stock exchange; we can watch its ups and downs in the "quotations" to be found in the world's general estimate of it.

These quotations, inscribed on every page of the newspapers, show us how it comes into competition here and there with other values.

For there are competing values: for example, *political power* (not always in accord with *mind*), *social security*, or the *State*.

All these values, rising and falling, constitute the great stock market of human affairs. On that market, *mind* is "weak" —it is nearly always falling.

Considering the mind as a value allows us, as with all values, to divide men according to the confidence they have in it.

Certain men stake everything on it, all their hopes, all their savings—all the vitality, courage, and faith they have managed to garner.

Others take only a moderate interest. For them, it is not a very exciting investment, its fluctuations concern them little.

There are still others who are almost completely indifferent to it; they have not put their vital money into the business.

And finally, it must be admitted, there are those who do their best to depreciate it.

You see that I am borrowing the language of the stock exchange. It may seem strange, adapted to spiritual matters; but to my mind there is none better, and perhaps no other, to express relations of this kind; for when you think of it, both the spiritual and the material economy can be quite well summed up as a simple conflict of *evaluations*.

I have often been struck by the analogies that arise, in the most natural way in the world, between the life of the mind in all its manifestations and the various aspects of economic life.

Once we have perceived the likeness, we are almost bound to follow it out to its very limits.

In both enterprises, in the economic as in the spiritual life, you will find the same basic notions of *production* and *consumption*.

In the spiritual life, the producer is a writer, an artist, a philosopher, a scientist; the consumer is a reader, a listener, a spectator.

You will also find the notion of *value* which I have just been using, and which is essential in both realms; likewise the notion of exchange, and that of supply and demand.

All this is simple, easily explained. These terms have just as much meaning on the internal market (where every mind argues, negotiates, or compromises with other minds) as in the world of material interests.

Moreover, in either case we may equally well speak of capital and labor. *Civilization is a kind of capital* that may go on accumulating for centuries, as certain other kinds of capital do, and absorbing its compound interest.

This parallel seems striking when we think about it. The

analogy is quite natural; I would go so far as to see an actual identity, and for this reason. First, as I said, the same organism is involved, whether in production or consumption—these terms always imply exchange; but more than that, all society is a result of the relations between a great number of individuals, everything that goes on in the vast system of living and (more or less) thinking persons, each of whom sees himself as both ally and enemy of all the others—unique as far as he himself is concerned, but indistinguishable and as though nonexistent amongst the many.

That is the point, and it may be observed and verified in the practical as well as the spiritual realm. On one hand, the individual; on the other, indistinct quantity, and things. So the general form of these relations cannot be very different, whether it be a matter of production, exchange, or consumption of articles for the mind, or of articles for material life.

How could it be otherwise? . . . It is the same problem in both cases: it is always a matter of an *individual* and an *indistinct mass of individuals*, in either direct or indirect relation; the latter above all, since in the majority of cases it is only *indirectly* that we feel external pressure in economic as in spiritual matters, or, in turn, exert our own influence externally on an indefinite number of listeners or spectators.

The result is a twofold relationship. Seeing that, on the one hand, exchange must take place, while on the other, men and their needs are diverse, what happens is that when these unique individuals, with their irreconcilable tastes or their abilities, industry, talents, and personal ideologies, come face to face on a market, whether of doctrines or ideas, of raw materials or finished articles, then the competition waged between their individual values forms, for a moment only, a dynamic equilibrium based on the *values* of the moment.

Just as certain merchandise is worth so much for a few hours today, just as it is subject to sudden fluctuations or to very slow but continuous variations, so with the values of taste, doctrine, style, ideals, etc.

Yet the mind's economy contains phenomena much more difficult to define, since most of them are not measurable, nor recorded by organs or institutions that specialize in doing so.

Since we are considering the individual in contrast with his fellows, we may be permitted to recall a saying of the ancients, that about tastes and colors there is no disputing. But in fact, the opposite is the case: we do nothing else.

We spend our time disputing tastes and colors—on the stock exchange, on innumerable boards and committees, in the Academies; and it could not be otherwise. Wherever the individual and the group, the singular and the plural, must come face to face and try either to agree or to silence each other, there is nothing but bargaining.

Here the analogy we are tracing is so striking that it borders on identity.

So, when I speak of the mind, I now mean an aspect and property of collective life, as real as material wealth and sometimes as precarious.

I mean to designate a kind of production and evaluation, an entire economy which either prospers or not, which is more or less stable like the material economy, which either develops or declines, which has its general powers, its institutions, its own laws, and is not without its secrets.

Do not think I am here playing with a mere simile, a more or less poetic device; I am not trying to proceed by mere rhetorical artifice from the idea of a material economy to that of a spiritual or intellectual economy.

In fact, if we look closely at the matter, we find that the opposite is true. *The mind came first*, and it could not have been otherwise.

It is the commerce of minds that was necessarily the first commerce in the world, the very first, the one that started it all, necessarily the original: for before swapping goods, it was necessary to swap signs, and consequently a set of signs had to be agreed on.

There is no market, no exchange without language; the first instrument of all trade is language. We may here repeat (giving it a suitably altered meaning) the famous saying: "*In the beginning was the Word.*" It was essential that the Word should precede the *act* of trading.

But the Word is no less than one of the most accurate names for what I have called *the mind*. The mind and the Word in many of their uses are almost synonymous. The term that in the Vulgate means *word* is translated from the Greek "logos," which means at once *calculation, reason, speech, discourse, and knowledge*, as well as expression.

Consequently, in saying that the *word* is identical with the mind, I think I am not uttering a heresy, even in linguistics.

Besides, the least reflection will show that in all commerce the first thing required is something to start the conversation, to designate the article to be exchanged, and to show a need. Consequently, it must be something that strikes the senses but is also intelligible, and that something is what, in a general sense, I call the *word*.

The commerce of minds, therefore, precedes the commerce of things. I shall show that the former also accompanies the latter, and very closely.

Not only is it logically necessary that this should be so, but it can also be demonstrated historically. You will find the proof in this remarkable fact, that those regions of the globe where the most extensive, the most active, and the oldest traffic in material goods has flourished are precisely those regions where the production of intellectual values, the production of ideas, works of the mind, and works of art started earliest and has been most prolific and various.

I would mention further that it is in these same regions that what is called *freedom of the mind* has been most widely granted, and would add that it could not have been otherwise.

When relations between men become most frequent, active, and numerous, it is impossible to preserve great differences of understanding between them, though differences of caste or status may persist.

Conversation, even between superiors and inferiors, takes on an ease and familiarity not to be found in places where relations are less frequent. For example, it is known that in ancient times, particularly in Rome, the slave and his master had a quite familiar relationship, in spite of the harshness, the discipline, and the atrocities that were legally permitted.

I was saying, then, that freedom of the mind and the mind itself developed most fully where trade developed at the same time. In every age, without exception, any intense production of art, of ideas, of spiritual values, has flourished in places that are also remarkable for their economic activity. As you know, the Mediterranean basin offers the most striking and conclusive example in this connection.

This basin is, in fact, a kind of privileged place, predestined, providentially marked out for the vigorous trade that grew up around its shores and moved back and forth between its ports.

It stands like a deep bowl in the most temperate region of the globe; it is especially favorable to navigation; it washes the coasts of three very different parts of the world; and as a result it attracts many and very diverse races; it brings them into contact, into competition, concord or conflict; it also stirs them to exchanges of every kind. This basin (which has the remarkable characteristic that a traveler can go from one point to any other point around it either by land, following the littoral, or by sea) has for centuries been the scene of both mixture and differentiation among various families of the human race, each enriching the other with every kind of experience.

There was found the impulse to exchange and keen competition: competition in trade, in ability, in influence, in religion, in propaganda, competition in material products and spiritual values at once—there was no distinction.

The same ship or rowboat brought merchandise and gods . . . ideas and methods.

How many things have begun along the shores of the Mediterranean, by contagion or dissemination! That is how all that wealth came into being, to which our culture owes practically everything, at least in its origins; I may say that the Mediterranean has been a veritable *machine for making civilization*.

And in creating trade, it necessarily created *freedom of the mind*.

On the shores of the Mediterranean, then, *intellect, culture, and trade* are found together.

But here is another example less commonplace than the one I have just given. Consider the Rhine basin, from Basel to the sea; and think of the life that has developed along the banks of that great waterway, from the first centuries of our era to the Thirty Years' War. A whole system of cities, all very much alike, was established along that river, which played the part both of a conductor, like the Mediterranean, and a *collector*. Whether Strasbourg, or Cologne, or towns nearer the sea, these great centers were built up under analogous conditions and showed a remarkable similarity in spirit, in institutions and functions, and in material and intellectual activity.

These are towns to which prosperity came early: towns for tradesmen and bankers. The network they form, broadening out toward the sea, is linked to the industrial cities of Flanders on the West and to the Hanseatic ports on the Northeast.

There, material wealth, spiritual or intellectual wealth, and freedom in the form of free cities were established and consolidated, and grew from century to century. Those cities were both strongholds of finance and strategic positions for the mind. They were the site of industries requiring technicians, of banks requiring accountants and commercial envoys, men specially trained and devoted to exchange, at a time when the means of exchange and communication were not very practical; but there, also, were to be found an artistic vitality, a thirst for learning, an outpouring of painting, music, and literature—in fine, the creation and communication of values fully parallel to the economic activity in the same cities.

It was there that printing was invented; whence it spread throughout the world. But it was along the banks of the river itself, and as one component of the trade generated by the river, that the book industry grew up and spread over the whole of the civilized world.

I have said that all those towns showed remarkable similarities in spirit, customs, and inner organization; they won or purchased a kind of autonomy.

There, wealth and the amateur met; the connoisseur was

not lacking. The mind, as represented by artists, writers, or printers, could flourish there in the most favorable soil.

It was an excellent soil for culture, which requires freedom and resources.

So that group of cities along the river gave rise to a narrow strip of provinces stretching toward the sea, quite different from the regions of the interior to East and West which were agricultural lands that remained for a long time feudal.

You must understand that I am giving a very summary account, and that to fill in the details of my sketch you would need to consult a good many books and rearrange my whole scheme of periods and places. But what I have said will perhaps be enough to justify my notion of the parallel between the intellectual development and the commercial, industrial, and banking development of the Mediterranean and Rhine basins.

What we call the Middle Ages was transformed into the modern world by acts of exchange—a kind of action that raises the temperature of the mind to its highest point. Not that the Middle Ages were, as they have been said to be, a period of darkness. They have their witnesses standing in stone. But those feats of construction, their cathedrals, those incomparable works by medieval architects—and above all the French—are for us real enigmas if we inquire into the conditions of their conception and execution.

In fact, we have no document telling of the real education of those *master craftsmen*, who nevertheless must have had highly technical knowledge to construct works of such scale and such extreme boldness. They have left us no treatises on geometry, mechanics, architecture, perspective, or the resistance of materials; no plans, no drawings, nothing that, for us, throws any light on what they knew.

One thing we know, however: those architects were nomads. They went building from town to town. It seems they must have transmitted their theoretical procedures and building techniques from person to person. The workmen and their bosses or foremen formed trade guilds, which exchanged methods of stonecutting and dressing, carpentry or ironwork. But no written document has come down to us on all those techniques. The famous notebook of Villard de Honnecourt is, as a document, completely inadequate.

All those itinerant builders, then, those carriers of the methods and formulas of art, were also instruments of exchange . . . but primitive, personal and, moreover, jealous of their secrets and the tricks of their trade. They guarded, as arcane, what any age of intense culture tends to disseminate as widely as possible and perhaps too widely.

There was also a certain intellectual life in the monasteries. It was in the shade of the cloisters that the study of antiquity was born, that the literature, the languages, the civilization of the ancients were studied, preserved, and practiced for several bleak centuries.

In the whole of the West, the life of the mind was terribly starved between the fifth and the eleventh centuries. Even at the time of the first Crusades it was not to be compared with that found in Byzantium and Islam, from Baghdad to Granada, in the realm of the arts, the sciences, and modes of life. Saladin must have been, in taste and culture, greatly superior to Richard Cœur de Lion.

Must not this glance at the high Middle Ages show us something about our own time? Culture, cultural changes, the value put on matters of the mind, the appraisal of its products, and the place we give to these in the hierarchy of man's needs—we know now that, on the one hand, all this is related to the ease and the variety of exchanges of all sorts; on the other hand, it is strangely precarious. Everything that happens today must be related to these two points. Let us look within and around us. What we may observe I have already summed up for you in my opening words.

I said that to invite minds to be concerned about the Mind and its fate was a sign of the times, a symptom. Could I have had such an idea if a whole mass of impressions had not been significant and powerful enough to make me reflect, and to turn my reflections into the act of expressing them for you? And should I have done so if I had not been aware that my impressions were those of many other people, that my own sense of a decline of intellect, a threat to culture, a twilight of the purer divinities, was growing stronger and stronger in all those who can sense anything in the order of those higher values of which we are speaking?

Culture, civilization are rather vague terms which it may be amusing to distinguish, contrast, or combine. I shall not dwell on them. For myself, as I have told you, they are a kind of capital that grows and can be used and accumulated, can increase and diminish like all the imaginable kinds of capital—the best known of which is, of course, what we call *our body*. . . .

Of what is the capital we call Culture or Civilization composed? In the first place, it is composed of *things*, material objects—books, pictures, instruments, etc.—having the probable life-span, the fragility, and the precariousness of *things*. But this is not enough—any more than an ingot of gold, an acre of good land, or a machine can be capital unless there are men *who need them* and *know how to use them*. Note these two conditions. If the material of culture is to become capital, there must also be men who need and know how to use it—

that is, men who have a thirst for knowledge and for the power of inner transformation, for the creations of their sensibility; and who, moreover, know how to acquire or exercise the habits, the intellectual discipline, the conventions and methods needed to exploit the arsenal of documents and instruments accumulated over the centuries.

I say that our cultural capital is in peril. It is so from several quarters. It is so in several ways. It is brutally so. It is insidiously so. It is under attack from many of us. It is being wasted, neglected, and debased by us all. The progress of disintegration is obvious.

I have already given several examples of this. I have shown as best I could to what extent the whole of modern life, often in very brilliant and alluring forms, constitutes a real malady of culture: by allowing that wealth which should accumulate like natural riches, that capital which must be deposited in successive strata in our minds, to be subjected to the general state of agitation in the world, a state both propagated and intensified by our abuse of all the means of communication. At such a pitch of activity, exchanges amount to a *fever*, and life devours life.

Perpetual shock, novelty, news; instability itself has become a real need; nervous tension is communicated by all the devices the mind itself has created. It could be said that there is an element of suicide in the feverish and superficial life of the civilized world.

How can anyone conceive of the future of culture—I mean anyone now old enough to compare what it used to be with what it is coming to be? I propose a simple fact for your reflection, just as it imposed itself on mine.

I have witnessed the gradual dying out of men of the greatest value for their contribution to our ideal capital, men as valuable as those who created it: one by one, I have seen our connoisseurs vanish, those matchless amateurs who, if they did not themselves create works, yet created the true value of works; they were the impassioned but incorruptible judges for whom, or against whom, it was a joy to work. They knew how to read—a virtue now lost. They knew how to see, how to hear, and even how to listen. Which means that whatever they wished to read, hear, or see *again* was, by recapitulation, turned into a *solid value*. And the world's wealth was thus increased.

I do not say that they are all dead and that no more will ever be born. But I note with regret their growing rarity. It was their profession *to be themselves* and in all independence to enjoy the exercise of their judgment, which neither publicity nor criticism could affect.

Intellectual and artistic life at its most passionate and disinterested was their *raison d'être*.

There was no theater, exhibition, or book to which they would not devote scrupulous attention. They were sometimes spoken of—with a touch of irony—as men of taste, but the species has become so rare that the phrase itself is no longer felt as a gibe. They are a heavy loss, for nothing is more precious to the creator than those who can appraise his work and who, above all, can appreciate the care he has put into it, the *work value* of his work, as I was saying just now—that appraisal which, with no regard to fashion or momentary effect, fixes the authority of a work and a name.

Today, matters go very quickly; reputations are quickly made, and vanish in the same way. Nothing lasting is done, for nothing is done with a view to lasting.

How do you expect the writer not to sense, beneath the appearances of widespread appreciation and attention to his art, all the futility of the age, the confusion of values and all the superficiality it encourages?

If he brings to his labor all the time and care he can, he does so with the feeling that something of this will take effect in the mind of the man who reads it. He hopes to be repaid by a certain quality and span of attention, for a little of the trouble he took in writing his page.

Let us confess that we pay him very badly. . . . It is not our fault; we are swamped with books. Above all, we are harassed with reading about things of immediate and violent interest. In the public press the news is of such diversity, incoherence, and intensity (on certain days particularly) that the little time we are able to give to reading, out of twenty-four hours, is entirely taken up with that, and our minds are left troubled, agitated, overwrought.

If a man is employed, earns his living, and can devote but an hour a day to reading, at home or in the bus or the subway, his hour is taken up with crime stories, nonsense, tittle-tattle, and invariably the same "news," in a confusion and abundance that seem calculated to bewilder and stultify people's minds.

Such a man is lost to books. . . . This is inevitable, and we can do nothing about it.

The consequence of it all is, first, a real debasement of culture, and, second, a real debasement of true freedom of the mind, for such freedom requires detachment, a rejection of all the incoherent or violent sensations we get so constantly from modern life.

I have just mentioned freedom. There is ordinary freedom, and there is freedom of the mind.

All this is a little outside my subject, but I must dwell on it for a moment. Freedom, that tremendous word widely used in politics (though forbidden here and there in the last few years), freedom has been an ideal, a myth; a word full of promise for some, threatening for others, a word that has stirred men and moved paving stones . . . the rallying cry of those who looked weak but felt strong, against those who looked strong and were unaware that they were weak.

Political freedom is almost inseparable from notions of equality and sovereignty; but it is seldom compatible with the idea of order, and scarcely more with the idea of justice.

But this is not my subject.

I come back to the mind. When we examine somewhat more closely all the kinds of political freedom, we think at once of *freedom of thought*.

Freedom of thought is confused in people's minds with the freedom to publish, which is not the same thing.

No one has ever been kept from thinking as he wishes. That would be difficult, unless there were machines for tracing thoughts in people's brains. It will certainly come to that, but not just yet, and it is one discovery we are not looking forward to. Meanwhile, then, we have freedom of thought—insofar as such freedom is not limited by thought itself.

It is all very nice to have freedom of thought, but that means we have to think about something! . . .

Yet, in common usage, when we say *freedom of thought* we mean *freedom to publish*, or else *freedom to teach*.

This sort of freedom creates serious problems: it is always raising some difficulty. At times the Nation, at other times the State, and again the Church, School, or Family has found reasons for opposing the freedom to think in published form, to think in public or to teach.

Such authorities are all more or less jealous of any outward signs of a man thinking.

I do not wish to deal here with the root of the problem, which is a matter of particular cases. It is obvious that in certain cases the freedom to publish should be supervised and restricted.

But the problem becomes very difficult when it is a question of general measures. For example, it is clear that during a war it is impossible to allow everything to be published. It is not simply that it is unwise to let out news about the conduct of operations—everyone understands that—but there are also certain things that public order itself cannot allow to be published.

That is not all. Freedom to publish, an essential part of the freedom of trade between minds, is also, in certain cases and certain places today, severely restricted and even, in fact, suppressed.

You see what a burning question this is, and how it crops up nearly everywhere. I mean, everywhere that questions can still be asked at all. I am not personally very much inclined to publish my thought. Anyone can quite easily not publish. Who forces you to publish? . . . What demon? And why do so, after all? Ideas can very well be kept to oneself. Why externalize them? They are so brilliant hidden in a drawer or in one's head. . . .

But, in fact, there are people who like to publish, to press their ideas on others, who think only to write, and who write only to publish. Such people usually venture onto the ground of politics. And that is where the trouble begins.

Politics, being obliged to falsify all the values which it is the mind's business to verify, excuses every kind of misrepresentation or omission that suits its purposes, and rejects, even violently, or forbids, those that do not.

What, in short, is politics? . . . Politics consists in the will to gain and keep power; so it must exert either constraint or illusion over minds, which are the source of all power.

All power necessarily wants to prevent the publication of those things not consonant with its exercise. It tries its best to do so. The political mind is always, in the end, forced to misrepresent. It puts into circulation, into exchange, false intellectual coinage; it introduces falsified historical notions; constructs specious rationalizations; in short, it allows itself everything needed to preserve its authority, which—I know not why—is called *moral*.

It must be admitted that in all possible cases *politics and freedom of the mind are mutually exclusive*. The latter is the *true enemy of parties*, just as it is of every doctrine that comes into power.

That is why I wanted to stress the different shades of meaning these expressions can take on in French.

Freedom is a notion that figures in contradictory expressions, since we sometimes use it to mean that we can do whatever we wish, and at other times that we can do what we do not wish—which is, according to some, the maximum of freedom.

This amounts to saying there are several persons in each of us, but since these several persons have only one and the same language, it sometimes happens that the same word (like freedom) is used to express very different meanings. It is a "word of all trades."

Sometimes we are free because there is nothing against what we are tempted to do; at other times we may feel more truly *free* because we have overcome an inducement or a temptation, we are able to act against our own inclination: that is a maximum of freedom.

Let us look for a moment at this notion, so fleeting in its

spontaneous uses. It occurs to me at once that the idea of freedom is not *instinctive* in us; it never comes unless it is called. I mean it is always *a response*.

It never occurs to us that we are free until something shows us that we are not, or might not be. The idea of freedom is a response to some sensation or suggestion of constraint, prevention, or resistance, something opposed either to an impulse of our being, to a desire of our senses, to a need, or to the exercise of our deliberate will.

I am free only when I feel that I am free; but I feel that I am free only when I imagine some restraint, when I begin to think of some state in contrast to my present state.

Freedom therefore cannot be felt, imagined, or wished for, except as the effect of a *contrast*.

If my body finds obstacles to its natural movements, its reflexes; if my thought is hampered in its operations either by some physical pain or some obsession or by the action of the external world, by noise, excessive heat or cold, some jarring vibration, or music made by the neighbors, I aspire to a changed state, to some deliverance, to freedom. I move to regain the use of my faculties to the full. I move to reject the condition that refuses me this.

You see, then, that there is some negation in this term *freedom*, when we go back to the origins of its use.

And here is the conclusion I draw. Since the need for freedom and the idea of freedom do not arise in those not subject to hindrances and *constraints*, the less sensitive we are to restrictions the less often will the word and the reaction called *freedom* occur.

A man who is not very sensitive to obstacles put in the way of his mind's freedom, to those constraints imposed on him by the public authorities, for example, or by external circumstances of whatever nature, will react only slightly against such constraints. He will feel no impulse to revolt, no reaction, no rebellion against the authority that hampers him. On the contrary, in many cases he will feel relieved of some vague responsibility. His deliverance, his freedom, will consist in the sense of being unburdened of the bother of thinking, deciding, and willing.

You can guess the enormous consequences: in men so insensitive to things of the mind that they are unaware of the pressures hindering the production of works of the mind, there is no reaction at all, at least externally.

As you know, a case is to be found not far away; you can see on the horizon the visible effects of such pressure on the mind, and at the same time you can see how little reaction it provokes. This is a fact.

It is only too evident. But I do not wish to judge, for it is not my place. Who can judge of men? . . . To do that is surely to be more than a man?

I mention this because there is no subject that touches us more closely, for we do not know what the future holds for those of us whom, if you will allow me, I shall call *men of mind*.

So I find it both necessary and disquieting today, to have to invoke not what are called the *rights of the mind*—these are but words; there are no rights if there is no force—but rather the benefit to everyone in preserving and sustaining the values of the mind.

Why?

Because the creation and organized existence of intellectual life have, at present, the most complex and yet the clearest and closest relation to life itself, to the whole of human life. No one has ever explained the real point about us men, and our peculiarity which is mind. Mind is a certain power in us that has involved us in an extraordinary adventure; our species has diverged from all the original and normal conditions of life. We have made the world like the mind—and we want to live in this mind's world. The mind wants to live in what it has made.

It was a matter of remaking what Nature had made, or of correcting her mistakes and so, in the end, of remaking man himself, as it were.

It was a matter of remaking everything insofar as man's means would allow, and they are already considerable; of refashioning his mode of living, equipping the portion of the planet he inhabits; of traveling over it in every direction, from top to bottom; of exploiting it, extracting its whole content of usable material for his purposes. All this is very fine, and we do not see what else man could do but this, unless he returned to a completely animal state.

But we must not forget to point out that a wholly spiritual activity goes along with this material equipping of the globe, and is linked with it. I mean the equipping of the mind itself, which has consisted in creating speculative knowledge and the values of art, and in producing a large body of works, a whole capital of *immaterial* riches. But, whether material or spiritual, our treasures are not imperishable. I wrote a long time ago, in 1919, that civilizations are as mortal as any living creature, that it is no longer strange to think that our own civilization can vanish, with its methods, its works of art, its philosophy, and its monuments, as so many other civilizations have vanished since the beginning—like a great ship going down.

In vain is it armed with all the modern means and methods of holding its course, of defending itself against the sea; in vain does it boast of its powerful engines; they propel it to destruction as easily as to harbor, and it goes down with all it carries, goods and men.

All this struck me at the time. Today I feel no surer than then. That is why I do not think it useless to recall the perishability of all our goods, whether culture itself or freedom of expression.

For where the mind has no freedom, culture sickens. . . . Beyond our frontiers, we can see important publications, reviews once very much alive, now filled with the most unbearable pedantry; it is obvious that all life has gone out of them, yet they must keep up the pretense of intellectual activity.

That pretense reminds us of what went on in the days when Stendhal made fun of certain learned men he had met: despotism had driven them to take refuge in discussing the commas in a text of Ovid. . . .

We thought such wretchedness was gone forever. Such absurdity seemed banished beyond recall. . . . But there it is, back again in all its force, in certain places. . . .

On all hands we find obstacles and threats to the mind; its freedom and its cultivation are contested both by our inventions and our ways of life, both by politics in general and by various policies in particular, so that it is perhaps neither useless nor unwarranted to sound the alarm, and to point out the perils that surround what men of my years have considered the sovereign good.

I have tried to say these things elsewhere. I spoke of them recently in England, and I noticed that I was heard with great interest, that my words expressed feelings and thoughts immediately grasped by my audience. And now, listen to what I still have to tell you.

I wish, if you will allow me to express a wish, that France, although burdened with many other cares, would make herself the repository, the temple where the traditions of the highest and finest culture may be kept alive, the tradition of truly great art, marked by purity of form and rigor of thought; and that she would also welcome and preserve everything that is highest and freest in the commerce of ideas; that is what I wish for my country!

Perhaps the circumstances, economic. political, and material, are too difficult: the situation among nations and competing interests, our state of nerves, and the stormy atmosphere that makes us draw our breath in anxiety.

But, after all. I shall have done my duty in saying so!

NOTES

Monsieur François Valéry wrote his introductory essay especially for this volume, and I am grateful to him.

M. Valéry is the younger son of Paul Valéry. Although not a diplomat by profession, he is an official of the Quai d'Orsay and head of the French delegation to the Organization for Economic Co-operation and Development. He has studied mathematics and English literature and has a keen interest in music and painting. M. Valéry studied music for some time with Nadia Boulanger and, at her request, became Chairman of the Fontainebleau Schools of Music and Fine Arts.

I am happily indebted to Miss Denise Folliot for her fine work and her sturdy tolerance as a collaborating translator; to Mr. David Paul for his brilliant touch in revising the translation and for suggesting a few excisions; to Mr. Bart Winer for excellent criticism and advice; to Mr. Richard G. Anderson for his help with economic terms; to Professor Jean Hytier, editor of the Pléiade edition of Valéry, whose "Notes" I have freely drawn upon; and to Madame Catherine David for her canny insights into the allusive and idiomatic turns in Valéry's prose, her indispensable contribution to the Notes, and for courage and wit in the face of deadlines.

The notes which follow are bibliographical and explanatory, by turns. The explanatory notes are not meant to supply general information. They are limited, with a few exceptions, to clarifying those allusions and other references which, though a French reader might be expected to catch them, an American or English reader might not. The bibliographical notes indicate for each work the occasion of its composition (when that is known), its first publication, and, if republished, one later collection where it may be readily found. The French title of each work is given after the English title. Except where otherwise noted, the place of publication is Paris and the publisher is Gallimard.

JACKSON MATHEWS

Preface, by François Valéry

xii. *Marcel Schwob*: (1867–1905), one of the remarkable younger French Symbolist writers of the 1890's, a literary historian and critic of great erudition, author of *Cœur double* (stories, 1891), *Le Livre de Monelle* (prose poems, 1894), *Spicilège* (essays, 1896), etc. Schwob and his wife, the actress Marguerite Moréno of the Comédie Française, were among young Valéry's closest friends during his early years in Paris. Valéry had planned to dedicate "L'Introduction à la méthode de Léonard de Vinci" (1895) to Schwob, but by a printer's mistake Schwob's name was omitted, and the dedication had to await the second edition (1919), long after Schwob's death. (See Gide and Valéry, *Correspondance*, p. 245; also Collected Works, Vol. 12, p. 186 & *n*.)

xii. *Kolbassine*: (Eugène), teacher of philosophy, a friend of young Valéry in Montpellier and later in Paris; they played chess or talked for long hours together. Kolbassine had a passionate interest in politics.

Of his break with Kolbassine, Valéry wrote in a letter to Gustave Fourment (Mar. 9, 1900):

> ... here is a good one: yesterday I got a letter from Kolbassine, full of insults—registered. I hadn't heard from him for two years. Then he saw my name with my little remark in the recently published list of subscribers for Mme Henry. . . . I answered him in three lines, calm and decent but strong.
>
> I regret this incident. It spoils a memory that was rather a good one, after all!

3. FOREWORD: "Avant-propos," written for the first edition of *Regards sur le monde actuel* (Stock), 1931; see *Œuvres II*, Pléiade (1960); tr. by Francis Scarfe in *Reflections on the World*

Today (New York, Pantheon Books, 1948); hereafter cited as Scarfe, *Reflections*.

5. *Horrible confusion*: in French the phrase *"horrible mélange"* echoes a passage from Racine's *Athalie* (II, 5) which most French children learn at school:

> Mais je n'ai plus trouvé qu'un horrible mélange
> D'os et de chair meurtris. . . .
> (But I found only a hideous mass
> Of mangled flesh and bones. . . .)

8. *Law of least action*: The principle of the economy of physical behavior, observed by Heron of Alexandria and others, but first formulated by the French mathematician and astronomer Pierre de Maupertuis (1698–1759). "The principle is displayed where the amount of energy expended in performing a given action is the least required for its execution" (J. R. Newman, *The World of Mathematics*, New York, 1956, II, p. 882).

It may be as well to make the general point here that Valéry's habitual use of mathematical and scientific terms had nothing vague about it. It was based on a clear understanding of their meaning, including a knowledge of their history. This point is nicely made in an article by Judith Robinson on Valéry's notebooks, from which I cite the opening passage:

The recent publication of Valéry's personal notebooks calls for a major change of emphasis in many of the generally accepted critical attitudes towards this most complex of all modern French thinkers. In particular, the *Cahiers* make it abundantly clear that nothing was more central or fundamental in Valéry's thought than his preoccupation with the methods and achievements of science, and especially of physics and mathematics. Throughout the whole of his adult life, the *Cahiers* show him reading widely and intensively in the field of classical physics, from Newton to Boltzmann and Maxwell, and studying with the greatest interest the development of mathematics from Euclid to Riemann, from Descartes to Gauss. They show him as well following in detail, and with tremendous intellectual excitement, the remarkable advances which were taking place in scientific thought during his own lifetime; the gradual emergence of relativity theory, quantum theory, atomic physics and wave mechanics, and the elaboration of abstract mathematical concepts of the kind embodied in group theory, set theory, topology and n-dimensional geometry,*

9. *Champ de Mars*: Valéry here uses the phrase in its general (Latin) as well as its specific (French) sense. The Campus Martius in Rome and certain Roman towns was an open level place where civic, military, religious, or recreational assemblies of the people were held. In Paris the Champ de Mars is the large esplanade between the École Militaire and the Eiffel Tower, where in 1790 a great gathering of the people of Paris celebrated the first anniversary of the capture of the Bastille.

18. *Temuchin*: the given name of the man whose title was Genghis Khan.

23. THE CRISIS OF THE MIND: "La Crise de l'esprit," written at the request of John Middleton Murry for the *Athenaeum* (London), and published first in English, in two parts: I. "The Spiritual Crisis," II. "The Intellectual Crisis," Apr. 11 and May 2, 1919; in *The Living Age* (Boston), May 10, 1919; in French, *N.R.F.*, Aug. 1, 1919; in *Variété* (1924); see *Œuvres I*, Pléiade (1957); tr. by Malcolm Cowley, *Variety* (New York: Harcourt, Brace, 1927; hereafter cited as Cowley, *Variety*.

On its first publication in French (in the *N.R.F.*), the

---

*Judith Robinson, "Language, Physics and Mathematics in Valéry's *Cahiers*," *The Modern Language Review*, Oct., 1960, p. 519.

essay was accompanied by this note: "*The Athenaeum,* the famous old London review presently edited by one of the most acute and distinguished men in England, John Middleton Murry, published in its numbers for Apr. 11 and May 2, 1919, two letters by M. Paul Valéry. Although these were written especially to be translated into English and for an English audience, we believe our readers will be interested in the French text, hitherto unpublished."

We later civilizations: "Nous autres, civilisations, nous savons maintenant que nous sommes mortelles." This is the most famous and influential of all Valéry's pronouncements, one of the great instances of modern rhetoric—comparable in power and superior in insight to Churchill's "blood, sweat, and tears." It has been endlessly cited and used; it served, for example, as the topic of one of the summer conferences at Pontigny, Aug., 1934. (See François Valéry's "Preface," p. xvi above.)

26. *Et cum vorandi. . . :* "When it has conquered devouring appetite, / Spirit will rule in triumph everywhere."

29. *Lionardo*: When Valéry, as a young man, was studying the Leonardo manuscripts in the archives of the Institut de France, in preparation for his first essay, *L'Introduction à la méthode de Léonard de Vinci*, he found in one of the margins of the manuscripts this note by an unknown hand:

> *lionardo mio o lionardo che tanto penate . . .*
> (My Lionardo, O Lionardo who hast labored so much. . . .)

He was moved by the intimate sympathy expressed by some unknown reader, whose hand left one in doubt whether he had written *penate* (labored) or *pensate* (thought). Or perhaps the doubt was an invention of Valéry's own mind—he used both versions. And he liked this strange old spelling of Leonardo's name. (See herein, p. 29; also, Collected Works, Vol.

12, p. 222 & *n*.; and Vol. 8, "Note and Digression," final page.)

Il grande uccello. . . .: "the big bird mounted on the back of his great swan."

31. *For me, everything relates to the intellect*: "tout par rapport à l'intellect." This is a deceptively *weighted* remark, modeled on one that Valéry attributes to Pascal in an early letter to André Gide (May 24, 1897): "Comme dit Pascal: 'Tout par rapport à Jésus Christ.'" Valéry means to say, in short, that the intellect is as much the center of his own world as Christ was of Pascal's. (See Gide and Valéry, *Correspondance*, p. 298.)

36. *Deminutio capitis*: "loss of prestige (or leadership)." The Latin phrase in its various meanings expresses one of Valéry's fundamental criticisms of the modern world. For another use of it, see CollectedWorks, Vol. 12, p. 76 & *n*.

37. A FOND NOTE ON MYTH: "Petite Lettre sur les mythes," first published as a preface to Maurice de Guérin, *Poèmes en prose* (Blaizot, 1928); in *Variété II* (1929); see *Œuvres I*, Pléiade (1957).

I cannot forgo the remark that this little essay has long seemed to me one of the wittiest and most intelligent pieces in all of Valéry's work.

43. *"In the beginning was the Fable"*: Valéry's essay "On Poe's *Eureka*" ends with this variation on John 1:1. (See Collected Works, Vol 8; also Vol. 4, p. 169 & *n*.)

46. A CONQUEST BY METHOD: "Une Conquête méthodique," first published as "La Conquête allemande," *The New Review* (London), Jan., 1897 (in French); first published in France, *Mercure de France*, Sept. 1, 1915; see *Œuvres I*, Pléiade

(1957); extract tr. by Anthony Bower as "Methodical Conquest," in *Selected Writings* (New York: New Directions, 1950); hereafter cited as Bower, *Selected Writings*.

This essay appeared in France for the first time during the first World War, with this footnote:

It was about 1895—twenty years ago—that English public opinion became clearly aware that the growth of the German Navy and the development of German industry and trade were threatening Britain's vital monopolies, or quasi-monopolies. Mr. Balfour and Lord Rosebery were the first to alert the British people. The principal text on the subject was written by Mr. Ernest E. Williams, under the famous title *Made in Germany*. This was a striking array of facts, and had a considerable influence. On the other hand, *Le Danger allemand*, by M. Maurice Schwob (editor of the *Phare de la Loire*), a similar book raising the same question and looking at it from the French point of view, went unnoticed and had no influence in France.

Toward the end of 1896, Mr. William E. Henley, a poet and editor of *The New Review* (in which Williams's articles had appeared), asked M. Paul Valéry to write an essay in more general terms on the developments in Germany. This study appeared—in French—in No. 92 of the London *New Review*, January 1, 1897; that essay is the one republished here. Though it is not our practice to include articles already published in French, even abroad, we do so in this case because it is interesting to show that twenty years before the events taking place today, there were a few Frenchmen who appreciated the "great soul" which the Germans have now displayed before an amazed world. Also, because the author's seemingly paradoxical thesis has now proved, beyond all doubt, true.

M. Henry D. Davray, in his "Lettres anglaises" (*Mercure de France*, Feb., 1897), commented as follows on this article: "M. Paul Valéry, in conclusion and with hair-raising objectivity, gives us a glimpse of the charming future in store for the human race as a result of the strict application of *method* in organization."*

*See *Œuvres I*, Pléiade, p. 1765.

The republication in 1915 of this early essay brought Valéry a number of letters. One was from the economist Victor Cambon, to whom he wrote in reply:

... That essay of 1897 was written, quite by chance, by an inquisitive young man who knew neither German nor Germany, and whose friends, wanting to help him to get published, suggested the subject.

It is true that the idea of method dominated his thinking. I have always resisted every kind of specialization—a fact I regret—but necessity drove me to organize my highly varied interests as best I could. Yet, once I had agreed to write a conclusion in French to Williams's series of articles *Made in Germany*, my difficulties had only begun. The subject was dangerously new to me. And I was in the hateful position of having to improvise, in order to carry out an *assignment* which at the time was very important to me. ...

The idea finally occurred to me to draw an analogy between military and economic organization. *In those days*, that was an arbitary point of view, a purely rhetorical approach. I meant to "fix" the truth, or make it fit, and perhaps at the time I did just that. In short, certain considerations of symmetry gave me the next *term* in the series ... called Germany.

This procedure made it possible for me to come to the point that really interested me. I did no more than touch on it in that article. I mean: method in the intellectual industry. Is such a thing possible? What would it consist of? Is it desirable? These are the questions I still spend my spare time trying to clarify.

It happens on occasion that I invade someone else's territory.

A few years ago, I drew up a plan for a thoroughgoing reorganization of our army. I saw in my mind's eye an organization with all its parts functioning so precisely that my imaginary army would have made our actual army look like a herd of sheep.

I spoke of it to a few officers; they were astonished, but nothing more. Since the Taylor system has come out, I realize that my army plan was vaguely like it. If I had been a German, I would no doubt have worked out my original idea and published it. It might even have been adopted and had some future. . . .*

In his interviews with Frédéric Lefèvre, Valéry gave this account of his meeting with Henley and his collaboration on *The New Review*.

I was very fond of London, which Mallarmé quite rightly called "a very engaging city."

I met the poet William Henley. Henley looked like a lion—tawny, gray mustaches, and an enormous face with a terrifying glare that from time to time was joyously transformed into immense bursts of laughter. In the years 1871–73, he had known many of the French refugees from the Commune, particularly Verlaine, with whom he had something in common, having spent long periods in the hospital. His French acquaintances had left him with a knowledge and love of uncommonly obscene language. He took delight in using with me, in French, the most outrageous expressions—of a kind he used far more sparingly in English. For the publisher Heinemann, Henley had founded a review which has since disappeared, but which had a good deal of political importance in its time. In this *New Review*, in 1895, Williams published a series of articles that aroused suspicion against Germany in English public opinion. It was as a result of those articles that England first became aware of the German pressure on the critical points of her economic life and her empire. The title Williams gave to his series was a great success: the three words *Made in Germany* were incorporated into law in a famous bill. At the same time they became fixed in the English mind, where they continued to be effective until Nov. 11, 1918. Henley had the odd notion of asking me to write for his *New Review* a sort of philosophical conclusion to Williams's work of observation and pure fact. I was baffled by such a task, which for several good reasons I was tempted to accept, but which *Reason* alone would have obliged me to refuse.

The "good reasons" had a numerical advantage, so I improvised

*See *Œuvres I*, Pléiade, pp. 1766 f.

what I could and gave *The New Review* an article that appeared in French. I called it "Une Victoire méthodique," but Henley preferred to give it the title "La Conquête allemande." The *Mercure* republished it in 1915 during the war. This essay, along with "La Crise de l'esprit" which I wrote for the *Athenaeum* in 1919, were my only efforts at a kind of political philosophy. This is a subject which, in the truest sense, is indefinite. I have happened at times to give some thought to it, always in an effort to find the characteristics and the simplest basic premises of the problem of politics in its *most general form*.

In this field there is a certain range of conditions and quantitative data which I believe are of decisive importance; but they are some-how too simple not to be quite often impossible to observe.*

Tarde venientibus ossa: "the latecomers get the bones."

47. *Mr. Williams*: Ernest E. G. Williams (1866–1935), English barrister and fellow of the Royal Statistical Society. *Made in Germany* (1897) was his first book. Other works: *Marching Backward, Plain Truths about British Trade* (also 1897); *The Imperial Heritage* (1898); *The Case for Protection* (1899); *Free Trade or Protectionism* (1907); etc.

48. *M. Maurice Schwob*: See note for p. 46, above. Not to be confused with Marcel Schwob, note for p. xii, above.

52. *"Enumerations so complete and reviews so general"*: the essential phrase of the fourth and last precept in Descartes' method (*Discourse on Method*, Part II, tr. by John Veitch).

54. *Landwehr*: German organized militia, equivalent to the United States National Guard or the British Special Reserve.

Landsturm: German home reserves, draft forces made up

*F. Lefèvre, *Entretiens avec Paul Valéry*, pp. 14–17. For a further account of the origins of this article, see "Current Recollection," Collected Works, Vol. 15.

of all those capable of bearing arms and not already in some other kind of military service.

58. *He threw his phlegmatic wig in the air on receiving a telegram*: presumably one announcing the Emperor's decision to mobilize the German army, which he was to lead in the coming war against France, July, 1870.

62. *Omni re scibili*: Pico della Mirandola, at Rome in 1486, called for public disputation of nine hundred questions and conclusions of his own devising in all branches of philosophy and theology—*de omni re scibili* ("about every known thing").

67. UNPREDICTABILITY: "L'Imprévisible," first published in *La Revue de l'économie contemporaine*, March, 1944; in *Vues* (La Table Ronde, 1948).

70. *"History is experimental politics"*: the French text here is "l'histoire est la politique expérimentale." Jacques Barzun suggests that this "slightly unidiomatic" phrase might be a French adaptation of E. A. Freeman's "History is past politics."

72. REMARKS ON INTELLIGENCE: "Propos sur l'intelligence," first published under the title "Sur la crise de l'intelligence," *Revue de France*, June 15, 1925; under its present title, as a *plaquette* (A l'Enseigne de la Porte étroite, 1926); see *Œuvres I*, Pléiade (1957).

This essay was written in response to a survey conducted by the *Revue de France* on the question "Is there a crisis in the liberal professions?" The inquiry was addressed to the clergy, the army, the universities, the press, and to artists and men of letters. When Valéry's response appeared, it was headed by this note, written by Marcel Prévost:

M. Paul Valéry has sent us a particularly important contribution. The author of "The Crisis of the Mind," departing from the particular subject of the inquiry and taking a larger and more general view, has chosen to deal with what he calls "The Crisis in Intelligence." It seemed appropriate that these pages should be published apart from the main body of the survey. In them, an important mind comes to grips with a problem of considerable interest today.*

87. *Sono lavoratore*: "I am a worker."

89. POLITICS OF THE MIND: "La Politique de l'esprit, notre souverain bien," a lecture given at the Université des Annales, Nov. 16, 1932; first published in *Conférencia*, Feb. 15, 1933; in *Variété III* (1936); see *Œuvres I*, Pléiade (1957); tr. as "Spiritual Polity" by Wm. A. Bradley, in *Variety*, *Second Series* (New York: Harcourt, Brace, 1938); hereafter cited as Bradley, *Variety II*.

During the 1930's Valéry lectured frequently at the Université des Annales (see note for p. 290). There, to the disapproval of a number of his friends, he reached a large popular audience. A note on this lecture in *Conférencia* indicates his hearers' response to "Politics of the Mind": "This lecture, with its admirable insight into our age and the chaos that characterizes it, created a sensation. The audience listened fervently, and time and again applauded the poet, the philosopher, the prophet—the revelations of the man whom André Maurois has called our modern Descartes."

103. *A recent piece of legislation*: there is little doubt that Valéry is referring to the application of "rational measures" by the rising Nazi Party in Germany, prescribing the elimination of the unfit and genetic selection toward the creation of a super-race. (See herein, note for p. 368.)

*See *Œuvres I*, Pléiade, p. 1771.

105—106. Exchanging a bird in the hand for a bird in the bush:
The French text here is "échange du *tiens* contre le *tu l'auras*,"
meaning literally "exchanging 'here it is' for 'you'll get it
later.' " Valéry's phrase is a variation on the proverb "un bon
tiens vaut mieux que deux tu l'auras." La Fontaine uses it in *Le
Petit Poisson et le pêcheur* (Book V, Fable III).

110. *Happy peoples have no mind*: a variation on the French
maxim "les peuples heureux n'ont pas d'histoire" (happy
peoples have no history). For another version with specific
reference to America, see herein, p. 227.

112. *Regulations to control copying*: copyright laws to prevent the pirating of "models"; enforced by the Chambre
Syndicale de la Couture, representing the principal Paris
fashion houses.

114. ON HISTORY: "De l'Histoire," first published as part
of "Grandeur et Décadence de l'Europe" in *Regards sur le
monde actuel* (Stock), 1931; as a separate article, dated 1928, in
Œuvres, Vol. J (1938); see *Œuvres II*, Pléiade (1960); tr. by
Scarfe, *Reflections*.

118. HISTORICAL FACT: "Discours de l'histoire," a speech
given at commencement exercises at the Lycée Janson-de-
Sailly in Paris, July 13, 1932, and published by Les Presses
Modernes, Aug., 1932. Valéry changed the title to "Le Fait
historique" (used for the present translation) in *Œuvres*, Vol.
D (1934), but reverted to the title above in *Variété IV* (1938)
and elsewhere. See *Œuvres I*, Pléiade (1957).

His sensational attack on history is one of Valéry's most
famous speeches. He had already expressed similar views,
however, as in the previous short essay "On History." (See
also Appendix II herein.)

The remarkable and thoughtful address we have just heard: Valéry was preceded on the program by Gustave Lanson (1857–1934), one of the great teachers of the century, Professor at the École Normale Supérieure and the Sorbonne. His *Histoire de la littérature française* has for several generations been the standard reference book on French literature in schools and universities everywhere.

121. *Your classmates in Philosophy*: "Philosophy" is the final year in the French *lycée*, leading to the second part of the *baccalauréat*, the diploma awarded on passing the oral and written examinations at the end of the secondary school program.

122. *Micromegas*: the hero of Voltaire's satirical, philosophical novel of that title (1752); he is a giant visiting the Earth from the star Sirius. (See pp. 223, 294, & *nn.*)

125. *Rhetoric Class:* a course in the humanities, originally including recitation and *explication de texte* of French, Latin, and Greek authors, with exercises in writing Latin and Greek prose and Latin verse. Before 1925, it led to the first part of the *baccalauréat* (see note for p. 121).

130. THE OUTLOOK FOR INTELLIGENCE: "Le Bilan de l'intelligence," a lecture given twice at the Université des Annales (see note for p. 290), Jan. 16 and Mar. 29, 1935; in *Variété III* (1936); see *Œuvres I*, Pléiade (1957); tr. as "The Balance Sheet of the Intelligence," by Bradley, *Variety II*.

Valéry wrote an earlier version of some of the ideas in this essay as a radio talk, given over Radio-Paris on June 12, 1934, and published under the title "Indication d'une politique de l'esprit" in *Les Cahiers de Radio-Paris*, Aug. 15, 1934; republished in *Vues* (1948). This early text has not been included in the present collection.

In this same place: at the Université des Annales. (See note for p. 290.)

150. *Baccalauréat*: the diploma awarded upon successful completion of the secondary school program. (See notes for pp. 121 and 125.)

151. *Rollin*: Charles Rollin (1661–1741), French educator. His fanciful compilations of Latin authors, *Histoire ancienne* and *Histoire romaine*, were among the first textbooks written in French. Voltaire and Anatole France both expressed a debt to Rollin.

153. *La valeur n'attend pas* ... : "Courage does not depend on the number of one's years," from Corneille's *Le Cid* (II, 2).

156. *And sometimes our masters' voice*: The French text here, "et parfois la voix de nos maîtres," is a complex pun on the Victrola trademark, "His Master's Voice," *La Voix de son Maître*, which is as well known in France as elsewhere. In French, Valéry's remark refers both to lectures broadcast by professors (*nos maîtres*), and to the speeches of political "masters"—a jibe at the broadcast harangues of Hitler.

160. REMARKS ON PROGRESS: "Propos sur le progrès," first published in *Lumière et Radio*, Dec. 10, 1929; tr. (anon.) as "Art and Progress," *Yale Review*, Summer, 1930; tr. (anon.) in *The Studio* (London), Sept., 1930; in *Regards sur le monde actuel* (Stock), 1931; see *Œuvres II*, Pléiade (1960); tr. by Bradley, *Variety II*; and Scarfe, *Reflections*.

The review *Les Marges*, in its issue of June 10, 1932, published an "Inquiry on 1900." Valéry's reply included, among other comments on the period, these on Progress:

In philosophy, minds were divided between two widely divergent schools: Poincaré with his Kantian ideas opposed to those of Bergson which were highly ideological and biological.

As for science in 1900, it would take too long to tell you what I think, though I was profoundly interested in all its aspects—without much time to devote to it. I would put first, above any other progress, the discovery of X rays and the work of Marconi.*

164. *The Ethnographical Museum*: in Paris, founded in 1880; its principal collection at first was the *cabinet de curiosités* of François I, exotic objects brought to France in the sixteenth century by foreign ambassadors and missionaries. Since 1938, this museum has been part of the Musée de l'Homme.

165–166. *Joseph de Maistre's celebrated saying*: "*Dites-moi, M. le Général, qu'est ce qu'une bataille perdue? Je n'ai jamais bien compris cela.* Il me répondit après un moment de silence: *Je n'en sais rien.* Et après un second silence il ajouta: *C'est une bataille qu'on croit avoir perdue.*"

("Tell me, General, when is a battle lost? I have never understood that." He answered me, after a moment of silence: "I don't know." And after another silence, he added: "It is lost when it is thought to be lost.") (From *Les Soirées de St. Pétersbourg*, 7th "Entretien.")

167. OUR DESTINY AND LITERATURE: "Notre Destin et les lettres," a lecture given at the Université des Annales (see note for p. 290), Feb. 17, 1937, first published in *Conférencia*, Sept. 15, 1937; in *Regards sur le monde actuel*, 1945; see *Œuvres II*, Pléiade (1960); tr. by Scarfe, *Reflections*.

168. *The Châtelet Theater*: the largest theater in Paris, seating 3,000; built in 1862; its machinery for quick scene changes and its elaborate sets and stage effects made the Châtelet famous for its fairy-plays and other dramatic spectacles.

168–169. *I was thinking of an old play of this type*: The whole passage that follows had been in Valéry's mind at least

*See *Œuvres II*, Pléiade, pp. 1552 f.

since 1895. In a letter to André Gide, Aug. 18, 1895, he wrote in great amusement:

> Such idiotic, fiendish tricks remind me of that wonderful curtain line in *Rotomago* (a fairy-play by Messrs. Clairville and Siraudin, I think). There's a fellow in it completely fed up with the magic tricks some sorcerer is practicing on his furniture. Just when one more inevitable trap is sprung, and the sofa fills up with water—no, wait, the room—the sofa turns into a boat, a sail shoots up, etc., the fellow shouts, "Here we go again with that stupid nonsense!" This line is irresistible, believe me! And it stays with me, I say it over and over to myself!—my sole verbal charm against the prodigies of print and bad luck—or luck—that keep cropping up. You can see how it applies to self-important people, books, sales. . . .

"Here we go again with that stupid nonsense!" (Curtain.)

173. *You never know what's coming*: the French, "la vie est faite d'imprévu," is doubtless a better proverb than our English translation.

178. *The Marais district*: that section of Paris around the Place des Vosges and near the Place de la Bastille. Many of its handsome seventeenth-century town houses are still standing, in various states of repair.

The Rue des Archives or the Rue Vieille-du-Temple: both are in the Quartier du Temple, once the property of the Knights Templars, and not far from the Marais district. The narrow, winding streets have kept something of their medieval air. In the crowded houses, independent craftsmen live and work, turning out *l'article de Paris*—the small, fanciful, often elegant objects in leather, beads, or feathers.

182. *Even Wells, in his famous book "The Time Machine"*: Wells's book (1895) had been the occasion for Valéry, as a young man, to publish some of his reflections on *time*, as a review of *La Machine à explorer le Temps* (*Mercure de France*,

May 1899.) See Collected Works, Vol. 13.

186. FREEDOM OF THE MIND: "La Liberté de l'esprit," a lecture given at the Université des Annales (see note for p. 290), Mar. 24, 1939; first published in *Conférencia*, Nov. 1, 1939; in *Regards sur le monde actuel*, 1945; see *Œuvres II*, Pléiade (1960); tr. by Scarfe, *Reflections*.

199. *The famous notebook of Villard de Honnecourt*: a thirteenth-century French architect whose sketchbook, preserved at the Bibliothèque Nationale, shows plans and details of Gothic cathedrals, landscapes, human and animal figures, and problems in geometry and mechanics. (See Otto von Simson, *The Gothic Cathedral*, Bollingen Series XLVIII, 1956, index, s.v.)

INDEX

[The letter *n* refers not to footnotes, but to those notes on the text which appear on pp. 212-230.]

This colophon was chosen from a number of drawings by Paul Valéry of his favorite device.